HANS ON IN HOSPITALITY

THOSE WHO SUCCEED IN THE HOSPITALITY
INDUSTRY ARE MADE, NOT BORN

HANS - RUEDI FRUTIGER

PARTRIDGE

Copyright © 2021 by Hans - Ruedi Frutiger.

Library of Congress Control Number:2021906001
ISBN: Hardcover   978-1-5437-6404-8
             Softcover   978-1-5437-6397-3
             eBook   978-1-5437-6398-0

Print information available on the last page.

To order additional copies of this book, contact
Toll Free +65 3165 7531 (Singapore)
Toll Free +60 3 3099 4412 (Malaysia)
orders.singapore@partridgepublishing.com

www.partridgepublishing.com/singapore

CONTENTS

Hansruedi Frutiger, a Swiss National started his career in the Hotel Industry in 1971, by visiting the Hotel School Lausanne worked as Waiter, Bartender, Cook, Front Office Administrator, Assistant Manager and Group General Manager

Over the years he gained cultural and work experience in various positions in Brussels, Paris, Basel, Zurich, Manila, Penang, Bangkok, Kuala Lumpur, Sharm el Sheikh and Phuket.

With his global assignments and inspired Management skills over the years in various positions at the Hotel Plaza Athenee Paris, the Mandarin Oriental, Manila, the Shangri La Rasa Sayang Penang, the Sukosol Hotels Thailand, and the Moevenpick Resort - Spa in Phuket.

He became independent traveler, coupled with great motivation and adventure, gained a lot of confidence and ambition and climbed the Hotel Industry as a great Leader.

He concluded his Hotel career in 2015 and started in 2016 as a Hotel consultant for the Dusit Princess, Kathmandu, Nepal.

If you have visionary Leadership and Entrepreneurial skills, good in Negotiation and Management, intergrade yourself as a good Team leader,set and achieve challenging goals, take fast and decisive action when needed, outperform the competition, and inspire others to perform at the highest level they can, that's when you have all the ingredients to be a great Hotel General Manager

MY JOURNEY – ROBOTS CAN NEVER REPLACE THE HEART

I would like to walk you through the ups and downs, the laughter and tears, the bitter and sweet in the Hotel Industry.

I hope to inspire young people like you, to work in the hospitality industry, where people serve people. It is a colorful career that nurtures a positive mind and heart, that opens doors and provides many opportunities to face unforeseen challenges and situations across the world, and in my case, from Europe to Asia. You need to be dedicated to the job and love various episodes in Life.

Robots may be the thing of the future, but do remember that robots cannot replace the warmth and personal attention to detail that we human beings are capable of. And robots most certainly cannot help to resolve personal problems should the need arise.

The hospitality industry allows you to develop yourself – professionally and individually. Not only do you improve on the professional skills you possess, but with time and commitment, you pick up other skills due to the variety of colleagues you meet, as well as clients and situations that will without fail, put you to the test.

Multiple characteristics are required for working in a hotel. These range from soft skills such as the ability to organise, communicate or work as a team; to more technical competences such as serving, revenue management, accounting and asset management.

Also, probably the most important matter is that you – literally – take care of people. This is debatable, but my experience tells me that it takes empathy and commitment to put another person's needs and desires ahead of your own, while keeping a smile on your face.

Customers come to hotels for various reasons, but in short, they want an experience. They want hotel employees and representatives to accord their time, care and attention. And just as people differ greatly, so does the care and commitment of each hotelier exhibited to his or her clients. Some may settle for meeting the basics, such as checking-in a family or serving beverages at the hotel bar, but others will take an extra step and not just meet their client's demands, but also exceed them. (Surprising them I feel, is the best method so far.)

With today's fast-growing businesses, more and more focus is channeled towards making a profit, which is the main purpose of business in the first place; however, in hotels, the products are not limited to events, meals, rooms or drinks – they extend to service and there is always a way to improve services and our service-industry skills.

Finally, the reason why I love hospitality so much is because it is simple, fun – as in enjoyable as well as meaningful if you get into it because you really want to. I love all the dynamics, and the shifting with different responsibilities and the feeling you have when you start training and end up in a managing position. It's more than satisfactory at the end of the day. And it does not stop with the customer-facing part of the hotel, you have the opportunity to meet and socialise with people representing a wide range of nationalities, in an even wider range of places all around the world.

In conclusion, the hotel industry is a pretty interesting and pleasant domain to get involved in. As with any other job, it has its ups and downs, and that's the great part of it: there is always place for innovation and there will always be innovators.

Before you read on, enjoy my video clips featuring some of my employees in 2013 and 2015.

Movenpick Mob Dance in Phuket
www. moevenpick Resort & Spa Phuket Karon beach flash mob dance

HOSPITALITY STARTS AT HOME

I was born in Basel, Switzerland.

My brother Lukas is 15 months older. My parents, my brother and I lived in a 2-bedroom apartment, in Muttenz, Baselland, Switzerland.

In 1955, we moved to a bigger apartment because of the birth of my twin sisters, Henriette and Barbara.

My childhood was quiet with traditional Sunday walks in the forest or listening to a dramatic murder case (play) on Radio Graz. One needed to memorise the story in order to follow the chapter in the following week. During my childhood, there was no TV available at home. Interactive communication, family reunions and friends were the main topic in life.

I believe that a happy childhood memory is essential for our well-being. Our parents were always doing their best to get us on the right track, sometimes not an easy task, to look after the needs of 4 children under the same roof. We did not have the luxury of engaging any helper.

My parents played a big role in our upbringing. Of course, there are genetic aspects involved. If the parents have mental health issues such as depression and anxiety, there's a possibility that the child may be predisposed to those issues as well. A stable home environment can go a long way towards off-setting those genetic disadvantages.

In my opinion, depression and anxiety are similar to diabetes and high blood pressure. Both are affected by stressful environments and can be improved with medicines. In many ways, the body and mind are interconnected.

The experiences we had as children set the stage for all the relationships we have in our life. The presence of our mother and father made the most difference in our childhood development. Children naturally want to spend time with their parents more than anything. Today, when a child cries, the task of pacifying the child is given to the nanny or to the iPad and other devices.

It is important for families to spend quality time together and engage in activities from swimming and mountain trips to vacations and ball games. These are the moments that mean everything to a child, making them feel safe, secure and loved. And when kids feel like that, they thrive, enabling them to become happy, healthy adults. The best part is, one does not need a lot of money to create such happy memories with children.

For us, cooking up lunches, dinners or desserts is a family affair. I have spent many hours in the kitchen to get to know how meals are prepared and this has strongly influenced my decision in entering the hospitality industry.

Family holidays that meant the world

In my family, weekends were spent outdoors. When it rained, we would play cards, Monopoly or watched an 8 mm black and white family movie of previous holidays in the Swiss Alps.

During the long school summer holidays, we went walking in the Swiss Alps and we loved Graechen in summer.

Graechen is an alpine resort in the district of Visp, canton of Valais. The village is located at an altitude of 1600 metres on a terrace above St Niklaus in the Mattertal north of the Mishabel group of mountains. Our parents loved to walk along the hills, up and down for miles. We would have our picnics on the way, and come back home around 5 pm and soon thereafter hit the sleeping bag feeling exhausted. We did not have any TV in the chalet that we rented each year. We played outdoors and enjoyed the fresh air in the Alpine region. My father owned, at that time, a 6-seater car for 2 adults and 4 small children and the luggage was always squeezed into the boot or placed on top of the car. I was always sick when driving along winding roads from St Nicklaus to Graechen. It was not my type of travelling. No safety belts were required at that time.

In winter, our holiday place was either Grindelwald or St Mortiz.

Grindelwald lies in the Jungfrau region and is only a short train ride up from Interlaken, the stomping ground and adventure capital for almost every tourist in the country. The little mountain village provides perfect access to two ski areas and numerous hiking trails. High above Grindelwald lies the Bernese Alps, and a famous mountain face. That mountain is Eiger's notorious North Face – yup the clothing company you have probably heard of, is named after a mountain in Switzerland. The highlight of winter in the Jungfrau region and Grindelwald has to be the ski and snowboard areas. Kilometers of pistes that are divided into three areas of equal pure bliss. There is Grindelwald First, Männlichen and Wengen and Murren, which are accessed only via a train. Most may head to Switzerland to take in the breathtaking landscapes, but we were after some fresh snow and great terrain. My parents had friends who lent us their chalet for 14 days, so we could ski the whole day and would feel tired in the evening after being in the fresh air for more than 6 to 8 hours. The slopes were beautiful and they still are. There were evenings where our parents would allow us to have some night life in the nearby bar and listen to some live music. As said earlier, we did not have any TV or handphones. It was pure family bonding escape.

St. Mortiz (Winter and Summer)

St. Mortiz is a luxury alpine resort town in Switzerland's Engadin valley. It has hosted the Winter Olympics twice, it offers the Cresta Run, which is a world-championship bobsled track made of natural ice, and an outdoor Olympic ice rink. Its frozen lake hosts polo, cricket and even horse racing on ice. Ski and snowboard areas include Corviglia, Diavolezza and Corvatsch, and there are well-groomed cross-country ski trails. The destination is expensive and meant for the rich and famous with some guests flying in on their private Jet to Samedan and being chauffeured to their 5-star luxury hotel. St Mortiz is a unique destination. If you ever get to visit this part of Switzerland, do enjoy a glimpse of luxury such as bobsleigh (Cresta run in St Mortiz-Celerina) or enjoy a hi-tea at Badrutt Palace Hotel where you can have a glimpse of the rich and famous while sipping champagne.

During our time, we stayed at the Laudinella Hotel, an all-inclusive hotel with classical musical performances at night. During the day we went skiing or walked through the forest. The cable cars and ski lifts at that time were priced affordably, but today the prices are on the high side.

Also, every once in 4 to 5 years, the entire Frutiger family clan would meet up for a weekend either in the Swiss Alps or somewhere in Germany. I personally did not enjoy this as the group was often too big and I did not know everyone. (Approx. 80 people would attend such special gatherings.)

On other occasions, during long weekends in summer, our family clan based in Basel enjoyed picnics in the Jura region, so there was again close communication between their children and my siblings.

The same group also experienced some summer holidays in Sark - one of the Channel Islands, near Guernsey and Jersey.

We travelled with a steam locomotive train from Basel to Strasbourg, changed platform to an electric train to Paris, boarded the evening train to St Malo and took the Hydrofoil boat to Sark. It was a long journey and the sea crossing the channel island from France to England was rough. My stomach would turn upside down and I would be as pale as a Japanese Geisha.

Sark: The smallest of the four main Channel Islands and located some 80 miles from the south coast of England and only 24 miles from the north coast of France. Not part of the United Kingdom nor the European Union, Sark is reputed to be the smallest independent feudal state in Europe and to have the last feudal constitution in the western world.

Whilst not strictly speaking a sovereign state, under a unique status, the Seigneur of Sark, the head of the feudal government, holds the island for the English monarch. Confused? Well, perhaps just a glimpse into the history of Sark will help to explain the unique status of this fascinating little island: The discovery of a few worked stone and flint testify to early life on megalithic or Stone Age Sark. Still later, it appears that the Romans inhabited the island, possibly for a few hundred years. The cousin of queen Elizabeth was the main person on the Island. We visited the 'Dame of Sark' who gave us some inside scoop on her living there during the Second World War.

In the mansion where we checked in, every morning a housekeeper brought to our room a cold and hot water jar to wash our face and other parts of our body. The whole family (usually 12 of us) would adjourn for breakfast and then we would go for a swim in the cold cave waters of Sark with a temperature of only 16 degrees Celsius.

The Sark beaches take little efforts to reach and they are worth the trouble when you are young and fit. Dixcart Bay is the easiest to access - via a cliff path with some steps. It's a picturesque sandy beach with an arch and cave and a walking path around the cliff top. Le Creux Harbor is a good place to swim, while Venus Pool, south of Little Sark is a rock pool the size of a swimming pool, accessed via tangled paths and is a spectacular place to swim and dive.

I remember when I was 10 years old, we enjoyed alcoholic duty free drinks in our hotel bar and the most popular one was a Pimms No.1 (I had a few sips and the world changed to become more colourful). The set dinner was simple and we also had the opportunity to meet the Dame of Sark who was reporting only to Queen Elizabeth II and the Privy Council in London. The security of the island was in the hands of two police officers; the jail accommodated two prisoners. The population was occupied mainly with farming and fishing, though tourism has become a growing source of income. Amazingly, the Dame of Sark had an electric car to drive around, while the rest of the small population, us included, went around the island on a bike.

Back to my home in Muttenz, Baselland

Muttenz is a municipality with a population of approximately 17,000 in the canton of Basel-Land in Switzerland. It is located in the district of Arlesheim and next to the city of Basel. As children, we went to primary and secondary schools in this town. We did not have any help for the daily cleaning of the large apartment. On occasion, we had the visit of a lady to look after us during the evening, when my parents were invited for dinner. My behaviour was on the naughty side when my parents were out. I showed my twin sisters (9 or 10 years old at that time) how to smoke cigarettes. We were clever enough to do it on the balcony so there was no evidence for my parents when they returned but they noticed this from the cigarette stumps found in the garden below, or from our breath. We were also sipping Coca-Cola at night, which I purchased secretly. My mother was strict when it came to sugar or junk food consumption, such as a Mac burger.

My mother worked as a headnurse at the Insel Hospital in Bern before she got married.

My Father was a Director at Firestone, a tyre factory in Pratteln (Baselland) near our home.

Traditionally, we all came back home for lunch.

After 5 years in the 3-bedroom apartment in Muttenz, 2 adults and 4 young ones, the apartment became small and so we moved to the hills of the 'Wartenberg' Baselland (the house was located next to the vineyards).

The more affluent people from Basel and the surrounding areas lived on this sunny hill. We rented this house with 4 bedrooms, 3 bathrooms, one dining area and a large living room with a verandah and a hilly garden overlooking the vineyards and Muttenz, and in the distance you could see Basel.

My siblings and I finished the obligatory 9 years of school in Muttenz, followed by a commercial school in Basel and for me, the hotel school in Lausanne.

Since my parents, especially my mother, practiced classical music during her upbringing, I was influenced and took up flute lessons for 2 hours every Wednesday for 8 years. I visited the Conservatorium in Basel. That was the time I was introduced to the world of classical music. I was then 11 years old and practiced weekly my etudes on the silver flute, learning the various intervals and musical notes. I ended my practice when I was 19 years old. Classical music from Bach to Beethoven, Telemann and Grieg. All were practised during the time at the Conservatorium. I participated once in a musical evening event and did win a prize, but a continuation as a professional flutist was not to be considered.

My siblings had no intention of learning any instrument. (Except my brother who took up the drum and played yearly during the Fasnacht (a carnival known as the 3 most beautiful days in Basel).

It remains unclear exactly why the carnival starts one week later in Basel than elsewhere in Switzerland or Germany.

The common explanation is that after the <u>Reformation</u> in 1520, Basel continued celebrating its Fasnacht, while the other regions officially stopped. It is said, that in order to differ from the Catholic customs, Fasnacht was scheduled one week later starting in 1529. There are no documents from this era supporting this theory, and the resolutions from 1529 were not quoted until 200 years later.

Today, the Carnival of Basel is said to be 'the only Protestant carnival in the world'.

In 2017 the UNESCO added the Carnival of Basel to the list of Intangible Cultural Heritage. It is a must-see when in Basel during the early part of March each year.

FROM A CAULIFLOWER DISASTER TO GM POSITION

When I was 20 years old, I decided to join the hospitality industry.

I loved serving people and mastering my knowledge in the kitchen, service, accounting and front office. Becoming the General Manager was my ultimate aim.

During Christmas and Easter season, I helped in various restaurants as a casual waiter for a small income. Later on, my parents registered me at the Hotel School in Lausanne, one of the prestigious hotel schools in Switzerland and around the world.

However, in the beginning, this was not what my parents and relatives were wanting for me to get into. The hospitality industry during the 1960s and 70s was not what was regarded as an intelligent profession with no good income. Why wait on others, work in the kitchen, work for long hours and be exposed to drugs, cigarettes, prostitution and alcohol?

The best hospitality school in the world

The Ecole Hotelier de Lausanne is hospitality management at its finest:

Switzerland's world-renowned dual education system, based on two key pillars, offers both academic and professional specialist education. Both the Swiss Professional Degree and the Bachelor of Science in International Hospitality Management are accredited by the Swiss federal government. The BSc degree is legally protected in Europe in compliance with the Bologna Declaration and is recognised as a HES-SO (University of Applied Sciences of Western Switzerland) degree. SSTH (College of Applied Sciences) and EHL (University of Applied Sciences) are the only hospitality management institutions federally recognised for their English language degree programmes in Switzerland.

Since 1966, many students from over 186 countries have graduated and are now internationally respected hospitality leaders. As we continue to strengthen our global Alumni Community, our close bond to the EHL Alumni Network – the world's largest hospitality network with over 25,000 members around the world – represents an exceptional opportunity in terms of knowledge exchange and career prospects. Not many of my colleagues from the hotel school pursued their career in the hospitality industry.

I also took a 3 months General Manager Course at the Cornell University in Ithaka, USA.

Living and working abroad

After completing all the apprenticeship in Switzerland, I went for my first assignment as a waiter cum bartender in Brussels, and completed a one-year assignment at the Hotel Atlanta, Blvd. Adolph Max.

The aim was not only to get the experience living abroad but also to refine my French language. The hotel was owned by a Gmuer family from Switzerland. I remember having a tough time finding a suitable accommodation. A German telephone operator working in the same hotel offered me an adjacent room in her apartment. As time went by, she invited me to share the room with her. Me not knowing that she had a relationship with a Japanese boyfriend agreed to her request and the rest was history.

One day, suddenly the apartment door opened and this Japanese friend of hers stood at the door frame yelling. I sensed some investigation taking place, and immediately left the apartment in a hurry before it became worse. I found an accommodation nearby the hotel but not knowing that in the evenings the tenants above and below me had some hourly clients and even offered overnight stays. My room door was mistaken with the visitors asking for unusual night practices. Laughter and other noises could be heard clearly in the corridors and staircase, again this was not the accommodation I was looking to have. To cut the story short, I later found my freedom with a quiet place to live in.

One year later, I moved to Paris for a 6-month apprenticeship as a waiter at the prestigious Hotel Plaza Athenee. There I served the rich and famous, actors, singers, politicians, couturiers such as Liz Taylor, Richard Burton, Gaddafi, Yves Saint Laurent, Ungaro, Karl Lagerfeld, Sophia Loren - Carlo Ponti, Hildegard Knef, just to name a few. As you know, Paris is a city of fashion, freedom, and love. My reason to stay in Paris for a couple of months was to be fluent in French. I was working as a waiter in a brasserie from 9 am till 2 pm and from 6 to 9 pm.

Once, a rich Parisian lady came for lunch at 1:30 pm and sat in my assigned serving station. I had an appointment outside the hotel at 2 pm and I asked my co-worker to look after her. He told me to work until I finished my shift at 2 pm and then go for my appointment. The lady knew what she wanted to eat and requested for cauliflower to be cooked in Vichy water. Since the hotel was so prestigious, all special requests by guests were honored. I was in a hurry and so I placed the order in the kitchen and got shouted at by the chef asking what I meant by cauliflower in Vichy water. I simply replied that it was as requested by the client. The appetizer and her beefsteak was cooked within the accepted time frame but the cauliflower took a little longer as it was cooked in Vichy water. Once it was ready, I took the silver bowl covered with a lid, placed it on a small plate with a paper doily to avoid it from slipping. I hurried into the restaurant and tripped over the edge of the carpet, just before the guest. The cauliflower in the silver bowl and the hot Vichy water landed on her legs. To this day, I can still see her clearly in my head, jumping from her seat, as the dish was hot, yelling to me in French and asking me to pay for her new silk dress. Thankfully the company absorbed the cost for the dry cleaning, but at that moment, I prayed that the restaurant floor would open up and I could jump in and disappear.

Experimenting with cooking

I practiced my cooking skills at the Restaurant Meditaranee in Basel. Typical of a new job to make mistakes, especially in the kitchen, I cut my fingers on many occasions. The loud noises and oily smells in the kitchen was not to be a prominent part of my hotel career and so I decided to continue in hotel administration.

The Hilton Basel opened in 1972 and I was able to continue my hotel practice at the Front Office followed by a period of time at the Hotel International in Zuerich – Oerlikon, both these two famous hotels are no longer in operation today.

Fulfiling my military obligations

Any young Swiss man 19 to 22 years of age who is fit to serve in the military in Switzerland must do this for 17 weeks (basic course) with a yearly repetition of 3 weeks until one is 50 years old or decides to go abroad. Upon my father persuading me to complete my military service to avoid getting into trouble, I complied and chose to be a cannonier. I completed the service with excellent notes and continued for another 17 weeks to become a higher-ranked soldier with a group of 16 persons to look after. I continued my military service with an additional 17 weeks as a fourier, where I was in charge of food and beverage for about 350 soldiers in the event of any emergencies. It was a learning curve working with a team, having to complete daily targets, wake up early and train physically. At 25 years old, I would say I was fit. I then left the military.

All soldiers get a full gear inclusive of a rifle with 18 bullets for any emergency events. Till today, the rifle has never been misused by any Swiss citizen who has served in the army to resolve any home disputes.

The automatic rifle is meant to be used in case of an emergency arising in the surrounding countries i.e. Germany, Austria, Lichtenstein, Italy and France.

Over to Asia

In 1978, I spotted a recruitment ad in the daily newspaper. The Mandarin Oriental in Manila, a newly opened hotel was looking for an Assistant Food and Beverage Manager. I thought there was no harm in trying and so I applied and got the job starting from May 1978. It was a long flight from Zurich to Athens, then Bombay to Bangkok and finally Manila. The planes at that time were not fit to fly 14 hours nonstop and needed to be refilled with kerosene. It was a tiring journey.

I was hired as Assistant Food and Beverage Manager at the Mandarin Manila in 1978 and occupied the same position till 1981. In order to maintain my work permit, I had to shadow (train) a local Spanish Filipino. It was a completely new environment for me, from the time upon arriving at the crowded international airport. The language, the culture, the food and just about everything was unfamiliar to me.

At that time, many 5-star hotels opened at the same time in various places in the capital and on some exclusive islands away from the city. There was the Manila Hotel, the Philippine Plaza, the Hyatt Regency, the Peninsula, the Silahis with its Bunny Bar, the Holiday Inn etc., all these names joined the industry. The hotels in Manila were all luxuriously fitted out, with drivers and porters and everything that a 5-star traveller would expect. The First Lady Imelda Marcos was actively promoting international conferences for Manila.

Many hotels were run by foreigners. During our morning briefings, there were 10 expats sitting at the table and 2 locals mainly the Financial Controller and the Human Resource Manager.

I reported to a German Food and Beverage Manager named Bernd Rottka. Our General Manger at the time was Juerg Tuescher and the Resident Manager was Eric Waldburger.

We had a great Kitchen Team with Josef Kuenzli as the Executive Chef and some other foreigners occupying various positions in the kitchen. It was an eye opener to be part of this luxurious hotel with so many employees. Labour cost at that time was inexpensive so the hotel could have 2 employees attending to each room.

The 5-star luxurious Mandarin Oriental Hotel offered 442 elegant guest rooms as well as a beauty salon and hairdresser. An example of contemporary architecture, this hotel opened in 1976, was fully restored in 2007 and was closed for good in 2015 despite the lease ending only in 2026.

We were serving many dignitaries, from the Philippines and abroad. We had many daily caterings to banks, private residences, and of course Malacañang- the Palace of Family Marcos. We eventually got paid within 90 days or longer. One good client of ours was Arndt Krupp von Bohlen and Halbach, (a well-known steel company from Germany, which was very active during the Second World War). Arndt married Hetty von Auersberg from Austria. He visited us annually with an entourage of 12 Philippine boys who also stayed at the hotel and were dressed in Barong Tagalog (a famous hand-painted white delicate shirt) by a famous local tailor.

Arndt was a very demanding guest and spent thousands of dollars in our hotel, not only in Manila but also at the Oriental in Bangkok. He owned many mansions and one of them was in Austria, where the movie Sound of Music was made. He flew on Concorde, the supersonic plane, almost on a yearly basis.

Arndt exchanged his family brooch with Imelda Marcos so he got the VIP treatment like a president. Sometimes he booked a private plane to a nearby Island. My parents witnessed this as I invited them to visit me in Manila.

An incident happened when Imelda invited Pol Pot for lunch at our 5-star French restaurant. Other guests noticed this and left the lunch table within minutes as they did not wish to be spotted in the same place where Imelda hosted lunch for Pol Pot.

Manila was an eye opener from the moment I arrived till the day I left in 1981. Everything from the culture to the language and the weather was new to me. (By the way, on occasion we had some earthquakes with one recording the highest of 7.2 on the Richter scale.) We had many brown outs, the so called no lights in the streets and in many households. Luckily the hotel had 3 good backup generators.

After my 3 years in Manila, I was offered a job in the same position at The Oriental in Bangkok but declined as it was not a promotion.

A headhunter spotted me and asked if I would like to join the Shangri-La Hotel Group in Penang.

I was offered a job at the Rasa Sayang Resort in Penang, Malaysia, in the capacity of Director of Food and Beverage from August 1981 till 1983.

The large resort is located on Batu Feringgi Beach, now called the Shangri-La's Rasa Sayang Resort & Spa. It offers spacious rooms surrounded by 30 acres of tropical gardens. It features two outdoor swimming pools in the Garden Wing and one adult pool in the Rasa Wing.

The hotel offers free shuttle services to the UNESCO heritage city of George Town, located a 20-minute drive away. Limousine airport transfers are also provided on request.

Rooms at Shangri-La Rasa Sayang have views of the sea or hills of Penang. They are spacious and decorated with wooden carvings and colorful fabrics.

The Rasa Sayang Resort has a 9-hole mini golf course, Eco Centre and Adventure Zone, which is a spacious play area for children located at the Golden Sands Resort, a sister company next door.

Guests can workout at the well-equipped gym or enjoy massages and treatments like aromatherapy at CHI, The Spa. As for the restaurants, the hotel features 3 restaurants, 3 bars and one at the beach front outlet.

I remember my first evening. I arrived at the resort after a 14 hours journey from Switzerland and was welcomed at the door by the GM. After checking into the room, the GM asked me to join him for a drink at the night club, which was packed with local guests. After some whiskey, I went back to my room. The next day, I met all my food and beverage supervisors, waiters and stewards including the chef who later on invited me for a drink in his office. Again some alcohol, which I am not used to when starting out on a new assignment, and so I declined the invitation and instead started getting familiarised with the new environment.

Later on, I found out that the GM and the chef were most of the time drunk at work and had used their expat privileges to the fullest till they were eventually asked to leave.

Many Westerners spend their winter at this resort.

We had weekly cocktail parties at the Rasa Sayang Hotel for guests who were big spenders or long staying.

In late 1983 during one of the cocktails, I met Kamala Sukosol Clapp, a singer and Thai entrepreneur who owns 4 hotels in Thailand today.

Kamala was impressed with my CV and asked if I would like to join her family's hotel business in managing the newly opened Siam Bayview Hotel in Pattaya in 1984. Since there was no other opening in the Shangri-La Group of Hotels at that time, I decided to join her as Hotel Manager. The hotel had 250 rooms, 2 pools, 3 restaurants and was located across the Main Beach road, and close to Holiday Inn, Grand Palace, the Montien, the Merlin, the Royal Garden and the Royal Cliff on top of the hill.

On weekends in the 1970s and 80s, Pattaya was the playground for the Thais and a preferred beach holiday destination for foreign visitors. The Americans visited Pattaya during the Vietnam war as their rest and recreation place. Sattahip was the Navy Airport where 52 Bombers landed and took off to bomb Vietnam in the early '80s. Today 'Sattahip Airport' serves as a low cost passenger terminal.

Once the Vietnam war was over, the town became a place of entertainment. Many hotels, bars, massage parlors and water sport activities started operation. The beach became dirty and the glamour of a clean destination ended in the sand. The locals only came to Pattaya when there was an international conference or a sport event.

The Manager Roger Koch at our sister hotel, Siam Bayshore in the southern part of Pattaya resigned and Kamala asked me to look after the other property as well. I hired a Resident Manager for each hotel and I got more involved in sales and marketing.

I travelled abroad on many occasions and did sales calls in Bangkok. I managed to sign seasonal accommodation contracts with tour operators for the 2 hotels. In 1986, Kamala decided to promote me to Group General Manager and I assisted her in the construction of the new Siam City Hotel in Bangkok located on Sri Ayutthaya Road. The hotel had 2 buildings with a total of 530 rooms/suites and all facilities of a 5-star hotel. Kamala engaged the well-known hotel designer Bill Barnsley for the interior. Bangkok has since grown with many types of accommodation and new residences.

Sukosol's hotel empire

Every family has stories... but this one is unique. Kamala is a visionary entrepreneur with strong sales and marketing background. I travelled with her to some Sales Forums, ATF, ITB or to Japan. (Later on, I travelled alone to get business deals for the hotels).

Here are some personal stories of the Sukosol family.

Backed only by her savvy intuition and dogged determination, she was able to build a hotel empire in Thailand. The Oriental Bangkok and Dusit Group of Hotels were always her goals to surpass.

As president of Sukosol Hotels, Kamala has overseen the building and running of five award-winning hotels in Bangkok and Pattaya. In her down time, she has raised four children, recorded a hit song and raised over 30 million Thai baht for charity. Her personal highlights include being named by Forbes Asia as one of its '48 Heroes of Philanthropy' in 2009; awarded the Medal of Saint Nicholas; the Wonder maker by the Russian government in 2010 and having the Order of Isabella the Catholic bestowed on her by the King of Spain in 2012.

Great privileges come with great responsibilities

The first thing that I needed to accept was that the wonderful privilege of running a hotel group came with heavy responsibilities. I guess that I was apprehensive and just a little frightened by the awesome responsibility that had just been handed to me. I was in a foreign territory and in a panic as to how I was going to control and direct this operation, the heads of department, the staff and the 3 hotels that seemed to be alive all around me.

As I thought of all the general managers (good and bad), that I had known on my way up to the top, I began to understand what my targets were in doing my best to be a good leader. More importantly, I understood that I was not alone. I had a huge store of knowledge all around me, inclusive of all my department heads, ready to be tapped into for solutions at any time.

I realised that the common attributes in all the good general managers I had, were some that I would need to adopt in my quest to excel as a General Manager.

While I had been given power, I realised that I could not use it as a weapon but rather as an opportunity to lead and create a better workplace for everyone. You cannot use power to demand respect. You have to earn respect by hard work and leadership by example. All the general managers that I considered good had all been humble, and hugely respectful of all their staff.

As a GM you are there to make decisions, improve the hotel both in results and operations, and lead it into the future. But this does not mean that you are above the rest of your staff, managers or line staff. On the contrary, to the guests, you are much less important. Think about that for a minute. For a customer in the restaurant, the dishwasher is vastly more important, since dirty dishes will ruin his meal.

For a clean and tidy room, you need good room attendants, not a great GM. For good food you need a good chef. The list goes on.

So, sitting in that office I realised that I was really at the mercy of my staff, and that I had to bring this 'orchestra' together by understanding their needs and expectations of me as their leader. I needed to deliver this if I were to succeed.

As a GM, I would only be successful if we all worked together to deliver a happy stay and deliver good value to our guests. To achieve that goal, I realised that we were all equal in importance.

No GM I have ever come across has known everything about his or her operation. Only the bad ones profess to have 'total' knowledge, which is an absurd notion. A well-balanced GM knows perhaps one or two departments in detail, and a little more or less about the other departments.

A good GM is one who is always learning on the job. A great GM is the one that is never afraid to ask for help and advice from everyone and anyone in his hotel. Let me assure you that room attendants know more about guests' feelings and their operation than any GM.

Dishwashers know more about the operational shortcomings in their department than any GM. Waiters know more about service efficiencies and service-kitchen problems than any GM. All that is needed to unlock this valuable information is a GM who is not afraid to ask.

Yet so many feel that it is beneath them or degrading to their position to have to go to an 'ordinary' employee for advice. It will make them look weak and ignorant, so they think. On the contrary, it will make them look much stronger and more confident in the eyes of their staff. It will earn more of their respect as an equal, as someone who is willing to learn from the staff that really do know the answers. I ate many times in the staff restaurants just to get the feel of the atmosphere and also taste the food. The employees appreciated this and gave me the thumbs up. Once a month, I also invited 11-line staff to join me for lunch in the main dining room and listened to their opinions. Their comments were noted down and shared with the department heads. Twice a year I had a town hall meeting to keep the employees informed of the happenings in the hotel, the achievements, the forecast, the expenses of the hotel and questions and answers were discussed.

I have always believed that a 'democratic' manager is better than one who is 'autocratic', although both can be successful. However, I firmly believe that if you are going to lead a successful and 'happy' operation as a GM, you need to treat people as your equal, show them respect, learn from them and earn their respect by example.

You are their boss, their teacher, their friend and mentor, but never lose sight of the fact that you are all equally dependent on one another to succeed.

Don't ever misuse your privileges. People are watching you and the management and owners are expecting from you, in meeting the bottom line you have agreed at the beginning of the year. If criteria are not met, one warning goes out. A second one will not follow as one's head will be on the chopping board. As a general manager, the salary and all the perks for a top job are well taken care of. Tax free, inclusive health insurance, car, business class tickets, 4 weeks holiday in a year plus the local holidays, food and beverage, school for your family etc.

In 1992, after Siam City Hotels and Resorts, I decided to visit Cornell University in Ithaca New York for 3 months to strengthen my knowledge in Finance, Human Resource and Revenue Management. I thought with this certificate in hand, it allowed me to get a leading posting in the US but since I worked in several hotels in Asia, my file always ended on corporate hotel desks either in Singapore or Hong Kong.

Expanding my experience in other parts of Asia

On my return from Cornell, I went to Hong Kong and tried my luck to go back to Mandarin Oriental or Shangri-La Hotels. Unfortunately, there was no opening for me. Once you leave a leading hotel company, there was no return. This was the policy at that time.

Ferenc Fricsay, a well-known executive from a search company in Hongkong, called me one day to join the pre-opening team of the Dynasty Hotel in Kuala Lumpur.

Dynasty Hotel had 788 rooms, 3 restaurants, large banquet facilities, 2 bars and roof top pool/bar. The hotel was located close to the Putra World Trade center and a main hub for large international and local conventions, and was also in close proximity to the Pan Pacific and the Legend Hotel. I went on sales calls to bring large conferences and exhibition businesses to Kuala Lumpur and the 3 hotels had a total of 1500 rooms and all the facilities to accommodate this kind of business.

My stay with the Dynasty Hotel as General Manager started in 1992 and ended in 1997.

Dynasty hotel is owned by Dynawell Corporation, a wholly-owned subsidiary of former listed company Gula Perak Bhd, which delisted in 2011, while Empress Hotel belongs to KSB Requirements & Rest Sdn Bhd – a 70%-owned subsidiary of Gula Perak Bhd. Tan Sri Dato Lim Cheng Pow was the owner of the Dynasty and had 4 children, all of them somehow involved in the father's business. Tan Sri had not only 3 hotels but also owned a construction company and was a majority shareholder in a 18-hole golf course in Klang.

I left the Dynasty Hotel in 1997 and in June 1998, I joined a Taiwanese, Local and Hong Kong company to re-develop Johor Bharu, in Malaysia, across Singapore. Johor was at that time a sleeping farmer's village. It was always a surprise to see a slow-moving town after crossing the bridge from the highly developed Singapore.

To do the above task, I had to form my own company, QMC Services Sdn. Bhd. (Quality Management Consultancy company). The take-off was very slow as we had to go through many red tapes in order to get the approval to build a new Johor Bharu.

The Asian Recession started in 1998/99 and the financial market collapsed. Unfinished projects were put on hold and only the Twin Towers in KL, the Putrajaya Government Head Office and Cyberjaya were able to be completed.

Since our project in Johor was put on hold, I had to look for an alternative solution and accepted a job as the General Manager of the Eastin Hotel in Kuala Lumpur. This was in early 1999.

I was in charge of the overall operation and profitability of the 388-room 4-star Business Class Hotel. It had 4 restaurants, large banquet and conference facilities, a well-established wellness center, and a night club. Heavy day to day owner's operation involvement made me look for a more suitable place to work.

Off to the Middle East (2000-2007)

An employment agent called me from Turkey and told me that there was a General Manager vacancy in Sharm El Sheikh.

At first, I hesitated to take up the challenge to leave Asia and travel to Egypt for a very different working place. I asked if I could visit the place first as to give me an idea of what it is like.

He told me that I could not ask for a free visit but to just accept the job for a good tax-free US dollar salary. I called a former colleague of mine who worked in Malaysia and later in Sharm El Sheikh at the Iberotel Grand Sharm to ask about the destination and the hotel. I found out that the destination was full of European travelers seeking the sun and enjoying the underwater world.

I must admit that it is a paradise for snorkellers and scuba divers. Crystal clear water, beautiful unspoiled reefs and only 4 to 5 hours flight from Europe. I accepted the offer for a change of environment and also to be closer to home as my parents were of old age.

The start at the Iberotel Palace (formerly Intercontinental Hotel) with all its facilities and well-planned back of the house area was not easy. The mentality of the Arab world is different to that of Asia. The culture, the religion, the language, the hot dry weather... It is a men's world as ladies could not work in the hospitality as they had to look after the family and could not serve alcohol. We had our own staff housing where most of the employees stayed.

I had 2 foreigners working with me and the other positions were held by the locals. The owner of the hotel was the President of TRAVCO Tours and Travel, the largest inbound Agent in Egypt. There was an agreement with TUI, the largest tour operator in Europe to send most of their clients to their preferred hotels first and later to the non-affiliated hotels.

The Iberotel Palace was located in the old market on a private beach and had an average occupancy of 85% YTD. ADR US 130 per month.

The hotel had 4 buildings with all having the sea view with balconies, a total of 255 rooms and suites, a small function room, 3 bars, 3 restaurants, 3 pools (inclusive of one indoor heated pool), a small garden and situated along the flat sandy red and brown sandy beach of Sharm El Maya Bay.

A charming hotel which, thanks to its subtle construction style and its exclusive furnishings, is an ideal holiday address for adults and couples who would like to relax.

It is a real treat for divers because the waters near the hotel is a genuine underwater paradise.

In the early stage, we offered only bed & breakfast and 1/2 board options, later when competition started it was converted to an all-inclusive hotel. (I had left by then).

As previously mentioned, I was lucky in regards of sales and marketing issues, as TUI was the biggest contributor to our revenue. My primary duties were to look after the guests' needs and the happiness of the staff, since they were the main contributor to the hotel obtaining awards from various travel agents abroad. The (TUI Hollies) supported me with happy guest comments.

Once the hotel achieved a certain percentage of happy guests at the end of each calendar year and was selected as one of the best 100 hotels out of 1350 contracted TUI Hotels, an exclusive invitation was sent to the GM.

One of the prizes was a 4 night's stay at the Adlon Kempinski Hotel in Berlin, sponsored by TUI Germany and only the best 100 hotels among the 1350 TUI hotels were able to attend the trip. One award was received at the Savoy London.

During my time in Sharm El Sheikh, I was able to travel and enjoy the country and culture of Egypt and the region inclusive of Lebanon, Jordan, Saudi Arabia, Israel and Syria.

There was one incident at the hotel where a fire broke out in the laundry room, which caused some severe damage to the exhaust and machines. Another one was a terrorist attack in 2005 in Sharm El Sheikh, which you will read in a later part.

Asia, still my playground

In early 2007, I had an interview with Mövenpick Hotels and Resorts in Zurich for a GM posting in Aqaba, (Jordan) or in Tunis. Both offers I declined as I did not like to continue in the Arabic Region. I felt Asia was still my playground.

After an interview in Mövenpick HQ in Zurich and Dubai, I flew to Phuket and accepted the General Manager position at the Mövenpick Resort & Spa Karon Beach Phuket.

It was in September 2007 that I joined Mövenpick Phuket as GM and stayed on until September 2015. It was a wonderful beach resort hotel with 336 rooms/suites/villas, plus 30 2-bedroom residences located on the beach front. It was owned by Prince Al Waleed Kingdom Hotels in SA. In 2012, it was bought over by TA Global Berhad, a Developer based in Kuala Lumpur.

The Mövenpick Resort and Spa Karon Beach located in the South-West of Phuket is a tropical sanctuary that offered 4 outdoor pools, 7 restaurants and bars and a well-designed spa.

The resort was just a 15-minute drive from the popular Patong Beach and Jungceylon Shopping Center. The International Airport was only 30 minutes away.

The spacious units at Mövenpick Resort Phuket feature modern Thai décor and beautiful views of the sea or garden.

Here are a few observations during my time in Thailand:

Thai staff are very friendly, outgoing, obedient, and will generally do whatever their boss asks them to do.

If they are told to stay late – sometimes many hours and sometimes without reward – they will. Staff will almost never disagree with their boss, at least not to their face, just as they will almost never offer suggestions on how things could be done differently.

To do so would result in the boss losing face – and that absolutely must be avoided. It is assumed that the boss knows best - that is why they are the boss, after all!

Thai staff play a very submissive role, doing as they are told, strictly following instructions.

Despite the fact that the workplace can be quite a strict environment with all sorts of rules and stiff penalties, Thai staff largely come and go as they pleased, often arriving late to work. This may incur a penalty, sometimes very steep, but that doesn't always motivate them to arrive on time. I have never quite worked out why this is so.

Thailand, while a fun place to work, is not necessarily where one is going to advance their skills or their career. It's a great place to spend the final few years of one's work life, a great place to work part-time and surely a fantastic place to be on a good expat package.

From Thailand to Nepal

In 2018, I was introduced to a lovely Tibetan family in Kathmandu. They asked me if I could be their consultant for a new hotel project in the Capital. I hesitated to take up the job as I recently retired and liked to enjoy travelling to new destinations I have not been. Eventually, I finally agreed and joined the family.

A little background on the hotel owners:

The Tibetan family comprised of the father, mother and 3 siblings (1 sister and 2 brothers) and together they owned the existing businesses.

This included 2 smaller hotels (Hotel Tibet & Hotel Tibet International) both located in Kathmandu. One hotel is under construction and renovation (the Hotel Lhasa) now called the Dusit Princess Kathmandu.

Some 30 years ago the father and his children left Tibet for India and later to Kathmandu. He set up a large carpet factory weaving silk carpets for export.

The 'Shangri-La Carpet' factory has been in the business for about 30 years. This industry has been producing the finest hand-knotted Tibetan carpets that were exported all over the world, mainly to the UK, USA and Russia.

The Dusit Princess Kathmandu, located in the north east section of Kathmandu in Lazimpat, is presently under construction and is only 8 minutes walking distance from the city center (Tamel).

The Dusit Princess is an upscale 11-story property with 108 various room types featuring every comfort for business and leisure travellers.

Due to the pandemic Covid-19, the opening date has been moved to 2023.

Presently the Dusit Princess is in a semi-finished construction stage. The interior decoration of various public areas and function rooms is not completed.

The back of the house flow has been carefully studied and has sufficient stores and preparation areas.

The 3 hotels are built and decorated in a prominent Tibetan style (very unique, compared to other hotel interiors). They all feature a unique content and formation of stone material on the outside of the building, window ornaments, and a brass roof top. Many wood carvings and columns can be seen in the building. All 108 rooms including suites are designed as such.

Most of the guest room furniture are fabricated in Malaysia. On the same level there is a large gym with equipment of international standards. Besides all the restaurant facilities, spa, gym etc., the hotel features a large roof top bar on 2 levels with an infinity swimming pool overlooking Kathmandu (a place to unwind).

BUILDING A GREAT TEAM STARTS FROM THE TOP

I climbed the ladder in the hotel hierarchy and acclaimed my first GM job in 1983 (31 years of age) and Group GM in 1986.

To me, effective hotel general managers should have a clear strategic vision for their property. They must consistently deliver or exceed the budgeted or desired financial results and at the same time, inspire team members to provide an exceptional guest experience that focuses on personalised services and memorable moments.

Every GM has a unique personality and management style. Some are autocratic while others prefer a more participative management approach. In my experience, it is best to apply a combination of both, depending on the scenario.

Here are the top five traits that are associated with a successful general manager.

Has No Ego

The Value Profit Chain counts and the best leaders achieve exceptional results by collaborating with their colleagues. You must realise that it is not a one-man show. Our business relies on great people, their personalities and passion for the job and making the difference. Trust is also crucial. A GM must be trusted by his team members to be effective. There is no room for ego either. Clever GMs surround themselves with highly-professional and effective people and they do not feel threatened by team members who are more accomplished. After all, it takes many experts to run a hotel effectively. The stronger the executive team, the stronger the GM, and this ethos filters down to other team members.

Good at Talent Spotting

GMs must have the ability to identify hotel team members with character and the right attitude, knowing that other skills can be taught. Employees with a positive mindset will learn very fast and they remain loyal when given opportunities to develop their careers. You must also give young high-flyers the opportunity to grow fast. Involving the millennial generation is essential as they are the future. General team members often think differently from more experienced General Managers, so it is paramount to engage them at all levels.

Setting a good example to all team members is important, as is delivering on promises. This proves that you care for your employees, guests, business partners, owners and the property itself, which must be treated as your home.

Brilliant GMs are the ultimate role models. You need to be passionate, committed, focused, trustworthy and decisive, listen to owners and management company as well as your people on all levels, treating them fairly and as equals. Patience is also essential, whether managing business relationships or implementing complex strategies.

Communicates Clearly

Effective communication is crucial, whether internal or external. Internal communications are best communicated face to face, in person. GMs should be open, transparent and address problems without delays, particularly in an age where social media can take over. Staging regular focus group meetings with all employees is important in addition to the daily MBWA (Management by Walking Around) as it makes a big difference to staff and guest engagement.

A good GM is aware of everything that happens in the hotel and can challenge the Head of Departments by understanding issues better and dealing with them faster. Daily briefings should be staged in the late afternoons to allow executives to attend to guests and hotel operations in the morning during busy times such as breakfast and check out. This allows the team to plan well for early arrivals and room allocations.

Must Have a Sense of Humour

A sense of humour can transform an average GM into a great one. It puts people at ease and makes work life happier and more fun. Humour can play an important role when navigating relationships with team members, guests, owners and other business partners. The top leaders display a high level of energy and drive and they never give up. If a door is closed in their face, they enter through the back window, because they always have plan B and C in place. This is part of the entrepreneurial spirit that defines an exceptional GM's behavior.

Always is Self-Motivated

And finally, the hospitality industry is fast-paced with changes taking place every day. To stay ahead of the game, as a general manager, you must be self-motivated, competitive and surround yourself with an effective team. You must also be practical. While academic processes and systems are part of our business, they can paralyse us, so it is paramount to keep things simple and exercise common sense.

The greatest GMs love their job, even though being in charge can sometimes make them feel lonely. Once again, to sum it all up, one must have a fantastic personality, remain humble and down to earth and never let one's ego get in the way.

Hotel business – Ups and downs

The hospitality business of the 70s and 80s is in many ways, unrecognisable from the environment we see today.

The change in technology, increasing labour costs (and decreasing staffing levels, multi-tasking with little training), increase of tourism and travel, and the rise of the hotel management companies, increase of stand-alone properties, RB&B just to name a few, have all played their part in the re-shaping of our industry. However, it is interesting to consider that at this point, the daily routines of a hotel General Manager are still very similar today to those of earlier times, only to prove little has really changed over the years.

It has often been said that no two days are alike for a GM, with the axiom 'people, product, profit' drummed in at a formative stage. This idea guided the activity for the week, month and year. The only real difference today as I see it, is the relative weighting of the '3 Ps' as perhaps there is far less emphasis on people (guests and staff) and far more on profit. Still, it is vital to achieve a high guest satisfaction index against the competitors. High employee satisfaction is also necessary or else a union will be formed, and of course a good Gross Operating Profit (GOP) as this will be taken into consideration at the year-end bonus for all employees.

It appears though that interference from owners seems to be a major factor that stresses many general managers because they are caught between their employer (the management company) and the owners of the property or in many cases an owner representative that parades his ego in front of the GM at every opportunity.

I recall a conversation with a GM who moved from an owner-operated hotel to an internationally-managed property, who told me that it took him 6 months to realise that he was not there to make money for the hotel owner, but for the management company! In today's world that includes a myriad of fees and charges, matched with complex management agreements, these can be two entirely different things...

This of course places the GM in an unenviable position trying to please both major stakeholders. Adding to this the rigours of 'servicing' owners & associated family members, management company executives demanding endless reports on trivial matters, as well as more mundane requests for the GM's time. It is little wonder why many end up hitting the bottle!

While still very junior in the management team of one luxury property, I witnessed one of those experiences where the fairly headstrong GM of the hotel had to deal with the owners and this incident has never left me. The old patriarchal owner himself was marvellous, but unfortunately his spoiled brat children had their egos and used every opportunity to show the GM who was boss! Today we have many new hotels in Kuala Lumpur and the children of the owners or even relatives are growing into the lavish surroundings and demanding what needs to be done.

Having worked in many so-called developing countries in the 80s and 90s, most of these GMs were often at the mercy of owners and sometimes the government. (I remember in one hotel in Asia we catered to high ranking functions and the police and army personnel enjoyed free meals. The invoice was paid only 6 months later and sometimes not in full, but this was the norm.)

So a day in the life of a GM was never dull, getting up at midnight or early morning to shake hands with VIPs or friends of the owners; having some corporate head office executive in the house who demanded constant attention; a suicide in room 412 or just simply a domestic dispute between a married couple who managed to demolish the room; entertaining travel agents – always on a free trip; or simply getting out the crystal ball to justify why the business wasn't as good as expected – of course no reason was ever acceptable by either the owner or the management company. I have experienced/witnessed a fire in the hotel laundry room, a bomb in front of the hotel and the escape of some culprits who did not pay the bill, you name it! All in a lifetime in the hotel business.

The solution for some GMs was to hire a good No. 2 and 'delegate' absolutely every part of the day-to-day running of the hotel to them whilst they patrolled the bar and restaurant delighting guests, accepting compliments for the exceptional job they were doing and no doubt drinking the profits in the process. They were the personalities that 'had' to attend every cocktail party in the hotel (and in town) assuming that they were not on the golf course by 11am or on their surfboard by 4pm – ah, all in a day's work...

But in their defence, it was always good to have a highly visible GM during those years – something that hardly happens these days because they are all occupied with writing reports, crunching numbers or replying to emails and social media comments.

Ah, the joys of 'full accountability and responsibility' in the life of the GM – (read punchbag for owner or Area Vice President having a bad day!). It's always good to have someone to blame for that poorly-designed kitchen, which was provided by the owner when they decided to cut costs by removing the cold rooms, or because of a budget shortfall due to the fantasy Gross Operating Profit (GOP) figure that the management company promised upon winning the contract!

Still the GM toils on, collecting a 'fair day's pay' for his 14-hour day. So what will the future be like? More of the same or will things start to change?

Will robots replace hotel staff and so eliminate the need for GMs as we know them? Certainly NOT. For many hotels, the GM is becoming a scarce commodity as GM clustering becomes the norm. Many are replacing the GMs with Resident or Hotel Managers to reduce expenses in the endless drive for more profit.

Ultimately it will be the guests who suffer from the commoditization of hospitality, as paying customers will have the final say on how far standards are allowed to fall before they act with their feet.

In the meantime, the GM will carry on doing his or her best to be all things to all people, a jack of all trades, until the next drama unfolds or when a report/request hits the email inbox…

A day in the life of a general manager includes working in the hotel industry while fulfilling duties that come with its fair share of challenges. Behind the glitz and glamour lies harsh realities that often go unspoken. The learning experience in various scenarios are priceless and lasts for a long time. Also, the various countries in Asia compared to Europe gave me a much broader view of what is happening behind the scene.

Sustainability- The way of the future

Sustainability is an increasingly relevant issue as it can affect hotels in many ways. These include improving brand image, as more customers are drawn towards eco-friendly companies and potential employees are looking to be part of companies that make a difference in the community; improving cost efficiency by implementing better working procedures and environmentally-friendly technologies that end up increasing the hotel's profitability. Simple changes such as recycling, installing low-flush toilets or going paper-free by investing in technologies that eliminate the need for printing or handwritten documents are some things that all hotels should be doing right now.

Customer satisfaction a must

Hotel guests are increasingly demanding and also more likely to give negative feedback on online rating sites when something goes wrong during their stay. Now more than ever, it's crucial for hotel managers to focus on improving guests' satisfaction by making sure that nothing goes wrong. The housekeeping and maintenance teams should be super efficient and make no mistakes. Housekeeping should have easily accessible checklists and failure reporting should be done as fast as possible to solve the problems instantaneously. This is a challenge, but it is made possible thanks to a maintenance management software that allows multiple people from multiple departments to report failures, which are then instantly communicated to the responsible employees or technicians.

Be it for failure reporting, instant check-in and check-out, replacing room keys or paying for leisure activities or meals, incorporating mobile technology into hotel processes for employees and customers is something that hotel managers must consider. This will ultimately improve customer experience and the hotel's overall efficiency and reputation. The staff plays a very important role. If they are satisfied with the work place and they get the support from the management, half of the daily demanding job is done.

Computerised Maintenance Management Systems are essential pieces of technology for hotels that want their maintenance teams to be able to solve any potential issues before they become actual problems for guests. This is definitely a challenge that gets harder as the years go by. Utilising online marketing that has relevant, targeted content is extremely important to drive potential guests to your website and, ultimately, to your hotel. Online hotel review websites, such as TripAdvisor or Expedia, are also very important. They can both help hotels secure new guests if they have quality ratings and reviews or drive every potential guest away if the reviews are poor.

A hotel's reputation depends a lot on these factors so it's important that hotel managers do everything in their power to get good reviews from guests (this should be done by giving them a great experience, not by pressuring them to do so!) and to maintain a strong online presence and communication on social media.

Customers are NOT always right

Whichever industry or product category we think about, personalisation is the word on everybody's lips. Customers are becoming more and more interested in products that they can customise or personalised experiences that seem to have been tailor-made just for them.

'WHEN ENCOUNTERING WITH DIFFICULT CUSTOMERS IN THE HOSPITALITY BUSINESS, ALWAYS REMAIN CALM AND COMPOSED.'

A career in hospitality can be highly rewarding, but sometimes you'll need to deal with difficult customers. First of all, the customer isn't always right.

We've all heard of the saying, 'the customer is always right', a phrase which was emulated by retail entrepreneurs like

Harry Gordon Selfridge. However, sometimes the customer is wrong and often this is because they had unrealistic expectations or had made a mistake.

The most successful hospitality professionals are proud of the work they do and are passionate about delivering exceptional customer service. Dealing with difficult customers can also help you improve your interpersonal and conflict resolution skills, so you can become even better at your job.

Here are some examples of dealing with difficult customers and how to stay professional.

THE FUSSPOT

- Customers who complain about the most trivial matters

Anyone who has worked in hospitality long enough will know that there are some customers who will never be satisfied, no matter how much effort you put in. For example, even if you were the highest-rated hotel or restaurant in your city on TripAdvisor, a fraction of your reviews (i.e. 1% or 2%) may contain a 1-star review.

You could do everything right, but you still won't be able to please everyone. That's just how it is in the hospitality industry. Even for the most trivial problem, it's important to stay professional and do everything you can to find a solution. This means you might need to keep giving the customer apologies for very minor issues – even something as trivial as the pillows not being the right color!

You may have to invite the customer to speak with someone more senior if they're still unhappy after you've made repeated attempts to resolve the situation.

THE EGOISTIC

- Customers who refuse to admit mistakes

Many people find it difficult to admit they are wrong. **Why?**

Because it is part of human nature and it can all be explained by what's known as cognitive dissonance. That is, people become stressed when they do something that is contrary to what they thought or believed, so they try to deny that they've made a mistake by shifting the blame to someone else.

For example, in a hotel, a customer might deny that they booked the wrong dates or the wrong room type because they're embarrassed that they made this error. Or, a customer whose card had been declined might insist there's a problem with the hotel's card reader – even though it's probably more likely that the customer's card has been blocked. As a hospitality professional, you must politely stand your ground and prove that the hotel was not responsible for these mistakes.

Undoubtedly, there will be times when you might make a mistake too – no one is perfect! However, if this happens, it's important to tell the customer immediately, apologise, and do everything you can to resolve the situation professionally.

THE IMPATIENT

- Customers who can't seem to wait or are easily irritated

Hospitality staff often has to deal with very high volumes of customers, particularly during busy periods like Christmas. That means people may have to wait in a queue – or they may need to wait a little longer than usual if a staff member is dealing with a particularly complex enquiry. Most customers are rational enough to accept this – there's no magic solution when demand outstrips supply. However, some customers might make a big deal about this by insisting that the hotel staff has deliberately kept them waiting, even though this is extremely unlikely!

In this situation, all you can do is to apologise for keeping the customer waiting (again, even though this is out of your control), and thank them for their hospitality even if they haven't shown particularly good manners. It's also important to explain to the customer why he/she has had to wait – i.e. you may be understaffed and/or the business may be unusually busy.

THE FOUL-MOUTHED

-Customers who resort to verbal abuse

A small minority of customers may fail to keep their temper under control when encountering a problem. However, no matter how unpleasant a customer's situation may be, you should never have to put up with abuse.

Firstly, ask the customer to calm down, tell them that you empathise with their problem, and reiterate that you'll do everything you can to resolve it. If that doesn't work, it's time to contact your manager. And if the abuse escalates, then you should advise the customer that you will have to call the security (if your hotel has this) or the police. There's a good chance that the customer will calm down before you have to make the call.

THE RIDICULOUS

- Customers who complain for the sake of complaining

Whether you work in a hotel, a theme park, or another hospitality business, from time to time you may deal with complaints that will sound so bizarre that you'd question whether they were genuine.

For example, a while ago, TripAdvisor posted 20 of the most ridiculous complaints made by holidaymakers – based on a research by Thomas Cook and ABTA. The findings were astounding. Here are three of those complaints (made by real customers to their travel agents!).

'The beach was too sandy.'

'We had to queue outside with no air conditioning.'

'We booked an excursion to a water park but nobody told us we had to bring our swimming costumes and towels.'

It's all in! Various platforms are used to complain and let the people around the globe know how they felt during their stay. It is always best to address the issue on site while on holiday or business.

There are also some interesting observations, which I would like to share. At beach resorts where there are Westerners, they tend to reserve the deck chairs as early as 5 am (to maximise their sunbathing) by leaving their personal items on the chairs and when they return, they discover others have moved their chairs to the front of their reserved chairs. To avoid conflicts, which happened a lot, I had to come up with warning signs stating that all personal items left on chairs will be removed after a certain time.

The Asians on the other hand like to cover themselves up to avoid the sun and prefer to come out towards the evening.

TRENDS – DEFINITATIONS – STRATEGIES

The internet is spreading not only into homes, but also into hotel rooms.

From access to streaming services to a room key on your smartphone, the essential hotel facilities in a guestroom are becoming increasingly digital.

Guests want concierge services or temperature controls at the push of a button (or tap of a finger), and voice-activated controls are expanding beyond simply asking Alexa to play your favorite song. These trends might sound futuristic now, but in a few years, guests will expect them. Many of these innovations require only minimal changes to a modern guestroom, so a forward-thinking hotelier can implement them quickly and efficiently.

Running a hotel successfully isn't easy. Hospitality management and operations is complex, with many interlocking pieces and dependencies. Hotel managers have to be great at time management, context switching, and problem solving. In a single hour, you may go from facing an unhappy guest to cleaning guest rooms, analyzing guest service requests, handling a plumbing emergency to interviewing a front office manager candidate to reviewing the latest revenue management report

The complexity and importance of a successful hotel operation is a frequent topic.

We're constantly seeking to deepen our understanding about the intricacies of hotel operations; then we identify ways for technology to streamline and improve operations and create content for our community around what we've learned.

So, whether you are new to the hospitality looking to learn or a veteran operator the platform of managing hotels is changing very fast.

Key Industry Terms & Definitions

A foundational understanding of hotel operations starts with defining key industry terms and concepts. A thorough grasp of these terms means that you can talk the talk and also know which levers you can use to improve a hotel's operations.

With key terms, such as RevPar, ADR, EBITA, GTS, EXTRANET, NET RATE, RATE PARITY, CUT OFF, STOP SALE, WHOLESALER, TA, LEAD DAYS etc., you'll be on your way towards building your successful hospitality career!

Front of the house: What's the difference between the front of the house and the back of the house? It may seem obvious but it's actually one of the most frequently searched terms when it comes to hotel operation. The Front; are all the Departments who are interacting with guests, (seen on the floor) the back of the house is supporting department for a smooth operation, sometimes not easy to define the various job description, as one feels this is not my job should be handled by the other person.

For example, a guest drops a bowl of food in the midst of busy morning hours, the waiter should assist the guest to get a new dish and must clean the debris from the floor, a cleaner should not be called at this time.

Hotel Room types. Did you know that there are many room types traditionally used by hotels? This can be quite confusing -- and not just for hotel guests. Hotel managers must also know how to market their rooms to guests, as room types have a direct impact on a hotel's market and price positioning. Best practice at the end of each working day to analyze a room sales report of the various room types and upgrades made. There is always a dispute between Reservation, Front Office, Sales & Marketing and Revenue Management for free upgrade, or undersell the room type.

RevPar: The hotel industry's top metric for evaluating performance is RevPAR. The metric combines occupancy and Average Daily Rate to track a hotel's performance, as well as a helpful benchmark to compare performance against a competitive set.

Hotel amenities: Today's guests are sophisticated and spoiled with choice. That's why amenities have become a key differentiator for hotels. You can create a virtuous cycle of higher guest satisfaction and better online reviews. In general, whatever the guest can touch, feel, experience he/ she will give you the Star grade. Don't forget the Human touch is the most important part of a successful hotel operation.

Hotel Brand guide: It›s hard to keep up with the number of hotel brands worldwide; the major hotel companies have been launching new sub-brands, each targeting a specific audience, at breakneck pace over the past decade. It shows brands from economy to Luxury brands, every large Hotel chain has this portfolio where the owner can choose in which category his hotel should be marketed.

Role-Based Tips for Optimizing Staff Operations

A hotel has staff with a variety of different jobs: housekeepers maintain rooms, front desk ambassadors greet guests, concierges make guests wishes come true, maintenance technicians keep things repaired and running well. And there are many other supporting Departments, all working diligently and collaboratively to keep the operation in a perfect manner.

Hotel Housekeeping department: Suggest you step into the housekeeping department for "a day in the life" view of what it takes to keep this essential department running at full steam, as well as the responsibilities, skills and requirements for each role. Effective housekeeping departments rely on software to keep everyone on the same page and to make dynamic room assignments / changes as and when guest check in and out

Hotel Concierge: The concierge is actually a powerful tool. Learn what a concierge does, and get ideas from a list of 35 things that your hotel's concierge can do for your guests, which can improve the guest experience and lead to better online reviews. He is the one who greets you at the door and he is the one who says good bye. He chats with you as you are waiting for your transport.

Hotel Operations Strategy

Operating a hotel requires not only a lot of organization but also a good measure of strategy. It's not enough to just schedule everyone and try to keep things from falling apart. Rather, you must implement strategies that incrementally improve your operations and allow your team to be more efficient (and happier) at work. These strategies will not only improve staff satisfaction but will also trickle down to a better guest experience across your property.

Hotel Checklist: Even if you hire the best people, you won't get the best out of them if everything is disorganized. To avoid a disorganized and inconsistent experience that frustrates your good people and drives them away, use checklists. Learn about the psychology of checklists and the areas that can benefit most from them.

SWOT Analyzes: By analyzing your hotel's strengths, weaknesses, opportunities and threats, you'll have a firmer grasp on your competitive positioning -- and which strategies and tactics are best for your hotel.

Technology has become a cornerstone of hotel operations. It's a superpowered ally, boosting daily operations while also showcasing your hotel to the world.

Team Wellness and Human Resources Tips

Hotels that consistently deliver a memorable guest experience share one thing in common: fantastic staff. As a hotel manager, one of your biggest responsibilities is nurturing a staff that cares deeply about their guests.

Minimum wage: Labor is always a top expense for hotels. And, in an industry that employs many hourly workers, it's fairly easy to have a gut reaction against raising the minimum wage. However, that's not necessarily the right reaction.

Stress is a terrible thing. Employees with high stress levels tend to call out of work more often and perform more poorly while at work. This "silent profit killer" must be tackled head on.

Hotel HR managers have a lot on their plate. In an industry with high turnover, there's always a position to fill, an interview to do, a new hire to onboard, performance reviews to file. It can be a very stressful job! But with the right technology, the job can -- dare we say it -- actually be pleasant.

As hotels gradually adopted more technology across all aspects of their operations, they became more vulnerable to hackers and bad actors. At the same time, the industry didn't necessarily do the best job at building layers of security that protect core systems. From guest Wi-Fi to public lobbies and online bookings, there are many ways that hackers can exploit vulnerabilities

The Cybersecurity: From ownership structures to global brands to international travel, the hospitality industry reaches across boundaries. This global footprint has real geopolitical considerations -- especially when it comes to data sovereignty, or where user data is stored.

There are so many different access points that hackers can use to gain entry to your hotel systems -- and it's not only the public Wi-Fi that leaves you open to attack. Hackers use all kinds of sophisticated ways to Pro for weaknesses and even trick your staff into sharing sensitive information.

Hackers love targeting hotels because hotels have a lot of personally identifiable information, such as credit cards and addresses. One recent data breach at Marriott put the spotlight on the industry cyber security practices (or lack thereof).

The hotel industry is not necessarily a first-mover when it comes to technology. Part of this is due to the inherent costs and difficulties of transitioning a 24/7 hotel operation onto a new platform, system or software.

One of the rare benefits to the ongoing pandemic is that there is downtime to reassess and potentially restructure your hotel's technology systems. Browse through extensive guides to see which hotel technology trends are influential and here to say -- and which ones are not living up to the hype.

What is an API: As one of the top trends of 2020, APIs are everywhere These Application Programming Interfaces enable different types of software to communicate, which is how you are able to build a technology stack that works for your hotel without having to rely on a single vendor or make compromises on functionality?

Cloud Computing: Arguably one of the biggest transformations in hotel technology has been the shift from on-premise hosting to cloud computing. By eliminating on-site maintenance and periodic upgrade costs, cloud computing can save money and keep hotel tech current and up to the latest standards. It can also increase speed.

Payment processing: One of the most annoying and confusing expenses for a hotel is payment processing. There›s no way of getting around it so you must get through it.

Maintaining control over labor costs is a critical skill for any hotel manager focused on bottom-line profitability. Hotel Effectiveness has built a system that can reduce operating costs with automated controls and instant alerts.

The Accounting in hospitality industry plays an extremely important role for recording the business's financial transactions. Without it, the financial health of the business cannot be known – In other words it's a life blood for a smooth business operation. (Departmental performances, Budget, Forecast, P&L, AR/AP Aging reviewing STR figures comparing with other Hotels in comp set and much more)

HOW A HOTEL IS MANAGED IS IMPORTANT. WHO MANAGES IT, EVEN MORE

There is a big difference between owner-managed and management by a company.

Defining the Hotel Operations Landscape: Owners, Franchisors and Management Companies

Running a hotel is no easy task, and to do it well, you need a diverse variety of skills and resources. To maximise performance, profitability, and the owner's preferences, many hotels use various entities to manage different operational aspects. Hotels generally fall into one of four ownership categories:

Privately owned and operated: For the owner, this model requires the most hands-on hotel operational work. At privately owned and operated hotels, the owner takes the lead on all aspects of the business: hiring staff, maintaining the physical asset, running a hotel marketing strategy and more. The owner could be an individual or an ownership group.

Leased: Unlike privately owned and operated hotels, the owners of leased hotels lease the physical asset to a different company who handles all aspects of the operation. The owner simply collects rent for the building and has no involvement in the hotel side.

Franchised: Owners who want a more hands-on approach and don't want to turn their physical asset over to someone else to operate might opt for the franchise model. Franchisors sign agreements with hotel brands for access to benefits (or limitations, depending on how you look at them) like brand standards, marketing power, reservation systems and design guidelines. Franchisors often run the day-to-day operations themselves, like hiring employees, handling payroll and they pay a franchise fee to the brand.

Managed: At a managed hotel, the hotel owner signs a contract with a management company to take operational responsibilities off their plate. Unlike the franchise model, the management company handles everything related to day-to-day operations including staffing, payroll and marketing. Some managed hotels are branded, and the management company is then responsible for upholding brand standards. The owner typically signs the contract with the brand owner, though owners often include their management company in rebranding discussions. These management companies focus on growing Revenue Per Available Room (RevPAR), Net Operating Income (NOI) and Earnings Before Interest, Taxes, Depreciation and Amortisation (EBITDA) as they are paid a percentage of revenue and often receive bonuses based on hotel profitability. 'Corporate' hoteliers tend to focus on more analytical tasks like SWOT Analysis and setting SMART Goals while 'on property' workers focus on tactics, day-to-day management and service delivery.

For a brand to have meaning in any useful sense, there must be a collection of clear and concise standards, which ensure that each user of the brand has the responsibility to deliver a consistent and uniform guest experience.

The great hotel operating companies of the world, whether they are international or entirely local, or whether they have one brand or a suite of brands, fundamentally depend on their owners and franchisees to adhere to brand standards.

Typically, the brand standards are most comprehensively codified with respect to five (5) star brands as these generally are the most treasured gems in the operator's stable of brands.

For both managed and franchised hotels, operators take various approaches to brand standard compliance. Some operators mandate brand standard audits and if it is not complied with on one or more occasions, then adverse consequences may be imposed upon the recalcitrant owner with the ultimate sanction being termination of the management or franchise arrangement. There can also be removal of the brand and the potential of a claim for significant damages against the owner for breach of contract.

For hotels under management agreements, compliance with brand standards at all times is achieved through the daily management leadership of the general manager and other senior personnel appointed to manage the hotel by the operator.

In practice however, operators adopt a common sense approach to compliance particularly with respect to matters such as upgrade requirements pertaining to technology. This is done in advance of the expiration of the life cycle or tax written down value of existing technology in the hotel.

To take but one example in the technology landscape, mandated requirements to comply with state-of-the-art plasma screen/LCD television receivers are tempered by a recognition that this should only be insisted upon when the life cycle or tax depreciation expiry date of existing television receivers is reached.

Brand standards are the essence of the symbiotic relationship between all owners and franchisees who are authorised to use the brand, and the operating company who is the brand owner. Each owner/franchisee looks to the operating company to mandate brand standard compliance across the chain of hotels using the same brand and to take decisive action with respect to instances of non-compliance.

The operating company relies on each owner/franchisee to comply with its contractual obligations to comply with brand standards and spend the necessary funds to ensure that this takes place.

I have had in many occasions either a visit of an appointed company by the management company or the owner, and have given them feedback on various likes and dislikes in the operation of that particular hotel.

The management company of every hotel typically engages a 'mystery shopper' 2 times a year to check on the operations of the hotel.

For example, the mystery guest calls Room Service for breakfast and on arrival of the tray or trolley, there is a 'Do Not Disturb' sign at the door knob. What would the waiter do in this case?

Or, during the night when everyone is asleep, the mystery guest walks the back of the house to see how the employees or security guard would react.

An overview of Airbnb

Airbnb is an online marketplace that connects people who want to rent out their homes with people who are looking for accommodations in the city or countryside.

For hosts, participating in this scheme will earn them some extra income through their property, but with the risk that the guests might do damage to it. For guests, the advantage can be relatively inexpensive accommodations, but with the risk that the property won't be as appealing as the listing made it seem.

KEY TAKEAWAYS

- Travellers can often book an Airbnb for less than the cost of a hotel room.
- The traveller risks not having the property live up to its listing.
- The host risks having the guests do serious damage to his/her property.
- The global pandemic due to the novel coronavirus has resulted in significant changes to Airbnb's Extenuating Circumstances Policy pertaining to cancellations.

The advantages of Airbnb

Wide selection

Airbnb lists many different kinds of properties: single rooms, a suite of rooms, apartments, moored yachts, houseboats, entire houses, even a castle, all on the Airbnb website.

Free listings

Hosts don't have to pay to list their properties. Listings can include written descriptions, photographs with captions, and a user profile where potential guests can get to know a bit about the hosts.

Hosts can set their own price

It's up to each host to decide how much to charge per night, per week or per month.

Customisable searches

Guests can search the Airbnb database—not only by date and location, but by price, type of property, amenities, and the language of the host. They can also add keywords (such as 'close to the Louvre') to further narrow their search.

Additional services

In recent years, Airbnb has expanded its offerings to include experiences and restaurants. Besides a listing of available accommodations for the dates they plan to travel, people searching by location will see a list of experiences, such as classes and sightseeing, offered by local Airbnb hosts. Restaurant listings also include reviews from Airbnb hosts.

Protection for guests and hosts

As a protection for guests, Airbnb holds the guest's payment for 24 hours after check-in before releasing the funds to the host.

For hosts, Airbnb's Host Guarantee Program provides protection of up to $1,000,000 in damages to covered properties in the rare event of guest damage, in eligible countries.'

The disadvantages of Airbnb

What you see may not be what you get

Booking accommodations with Airbnb is not like booking a room with a major hotel chain, where you have a reasonable assurance that the property will be as advertised. Individual hosts create their own listings, and some may be more honest than others. However, previous guests often post comments about their experiences, which can provide a more objective view.

It is always wise to check the comments of other guests who have stayed at that Airbnb property to make sure the listing is accurate.

Potential damage

The biggest risk for hosts is probably the possibility of their property getting damaged. While most stays go without incidents, there are stories of entire houses being trashed by dozens of partygoers when the Airbnb hosts thought they were renting to a quiet family. Airbnb's Host Guarantee Program, as described above, provides some assurance, but it may not cover everything, such as cash, rare artwork, jewelry, and pets. Hosts whose homes are damaged may also experience considerable inconvenience.

Add-on fees

Airbnb imposes a number of additional fees (as, of course, do hotels and other lodging providers). Guests pay a guest service fee of 0% to 20% on top of the reservation fee, to cover Airbnb's customer support and other services. Prices are displayed in the currency the user selects, provided Airbnb supports it. Banks or credit card issuers may add fees if applicable.

And while listings are free, Airbnb charges hosts a service fee of at least 3% for each reservation, to cover the cost of processing the transaction.

Taxes

Airbnb does not pay taxes to the tourism association.

WARM HUMAN WAKE UP CALLS TO AUTO VOICE COMMANDS

During my apprentice time in Switzerland and abroad, we had no fax machine, computers or emails. Back then, we used a telex machine to communicate and typed on electric IBM typewriters, where on occasion we used white liquid ink to erase mistakes on letters. The letters were all copied by using sticky black carbon papers.

The check-in and check-out processes at many front desks were done manually. In the evenings, we had to capture the guests' data from their registration cards i.e. the country of origin, nationality, length of stay, purpose of stay (business or pleasure), single or twin occupancy and the agent's name if any. After the change of shifts, we had to compare our check-in and check-out details with the front office cashier to see if all guests were registered, indicate if the room's price per night was matching with the agreement and how the guest was going to settle the bill upon checking out.

The telephone operator had to rearrange the information according to the alphabet from A to Z and had to check the correctness of the names and room numbers. All details were typed on the folio and a ticket was distributed to the concierge, the telephone operator, the front office and the cashier. We communicated by phone and beeper with the line staff of housekeeping, the engineer and other head of departments when there was any need for help.

Technology has definitely changed our lives. I remember in 1984, I sent my first fax to an overseas travel agent and was surprised that he was able to read my message and reply on the same paper. Today, personal computers, mobile phones, CCTV cameras, GPS systems among other forms of technology have directly impacted the human life.

The Internet in particular, has revolutionised human experiences and can impact human life in both positive and negative ways. Let's evaluate the positives and negatives in which technology has impacted human life.

A few decades ago, the Internet was just emerging and different groups of people and organisations reacted differently to the Internet idea. Some saw an opportunity to reach the entire world to expand their business markets, and to get in touch with family and friends across the world. Other people were cautious at first, pointing to the increase in the spread of official evils such as pornography and crime.

I had my first computer lessons in 1987 on an IBM desktop with an external disk drive. Later I bought a heavy laptop and a Nokia handphone without a camera.

In the current world, technology has grown even more with new inventions in major sectors. One of the most important changes that technology has brought to human life is communication. Individuals can communicate across the world in real time. This convenience is led by Google and Zoom.

Smartphones have taken communication to a whole new level. Instead of picking a phone to call someone or going over to distant places to chat, smartphones have made it possible for people to hold virtual chats.

I remember in 1960 when we tried to call from Switzerland to England, we had to ask the exchange office to connect us on a certain day at a certain time.

Social media has made communication even simpler and more efficient. Such sites as Facebook, Twitter, Instagram, Snapchat and many others enable people to instantly share information including news, pictures and videos. An event occurring in a remote place in China or on a mountain in Vietnam, is related live and the whole world gets to know about it and to see photos without waiting for traditional media houses to deliver such information. Information is more readily available than in the past. Greeting cards are gone and mobile phones have taken over.

Businesses have benefited from these changes immensely. I think we can no longer live without such technologies.

Many firms have cut costs and experienced steady growth in their sales revenue due to a reduction in the number of people required to perform certain tasks. Robots and machines that are capable of interacting with people have taken over key operations. Employees can work from home, giving them more freedom.

Video conferencing for instance has made it possible for people to cut on time and travelling costs. Meetings involving participants across different parts of the world can be held online. Online banking has made it easier for people to carry out financial services from the safety of their homes and to pay for goods and services at physical and online stores without necessarily carrying cash. Tesco delivers to your doorstep, meals are ordered online and delivered, credit cards are used to buy coffee in Starbucks and other outlets. We walk around with less cash. In China, it is so advanced that even the open markets accept only cards as payment. "Do you want for us to swipe the card?", is the usual question from the seller.

When booking a vacation trip, everything is done today via the Internet, from flights to hotels, renting a car and hiring guides, all is done through the computer. I have done long distance travelling with friends and all have worked well. Just a little more work from home, but cheaper than engaging an agent. However, care needs to be practiced when using this platform as you can fall into the red financially or lose your time replying to fake news.

Online dating has become a common phenomenon. A man in Pakistan can date ten prospects from ten different countries, and set up an online meeting with each of them. It could lead or mislead to a marriage.

The rate at which readers use physical libraries has decreased tremendously due to the availability of digital devices where one can read books on smartphones, e-readers, and tablets.

Online learning has made it possible for students to touch on education from across the world. Additionally, TV and radio experiences have changed significantly. No one has to remain a prisoner to their TV set as televisions and radios are also integrated into smartphones, tablets and even laptops.

GPS services have made driving easier and CCTV cameras have intensified surveillance. Also, newer technologies such as artificial intelligence and 3D printing have added to human independence. Soon, 5G will be in the market and we will be tracked wherever we go and whatever we do.

On the other hand, technology is also eroding the human species. Pornography has become rampant, and this is perpetuated by the Internet, which is readily available all over the world. With the Internet, pornography is accessible through various devices including the mobile phone. This is a phenomenon that breaks up marriages, and at the same time intensifies moral decadence. Human trafficking, prostitution, drug trafficking and other social evils have been facilitated by the technology today.

In the 21st century, terrorism stands out as one of the greatest threats to human life. Terrorist groups have turned to the Internet to spread their message of hatred and violence. They recruit followers all over the world through specific websites and social media forums. Cybercrime has also become a new threat to the world. Depositors' bank accounts are now more vulnerable than before, and billions of dollars are lost annually due to these crimes.

I was also hacked. Cybercrime perpetuates racism and hatred as hackers spread negative, devastating social, political and religious messages to their targets. Furthermore, human intelligence shown by robots poses a threat to the human race.

It is argued that robots will, at one time, completely phase out the role of humans. Where will we go from there?

The Hotel Industry: Then and now

From antiquity to the Middle Ages - The history of hotels is intimately connected to that of civilisations. Or rather, it is a part of that history. Facilities offering guests hospitality have been in evidence since early biblical times.

The Greeks developed thermal baths in villages designed for rest and recuperation. Later, the Romans built mansions to provide accommodation for travellers on government business. The Romans were the first to develop thermal baths in England, Switzerland and the Middle East. Later on, caravanserais appeared, providing a resting place for caravans along Middle Eastern routes. In the Middle Ages, monasteries and abbeys were the first establishments to offer refuge to travellers on a regular basis. Religious orders also built inns, hospices and hospitals to cater for those on the move.

Inns multiplied, but they did not yet offer meals. Staging posts were established for governmental transports and as rest stops. They provided shelter and allowed horses to be changed more easily. Numerous refuges then sprang up for pilgrims and crusaders on their way to the Holy Land.

In Switzerland in the 1800s, patients with lung disease such as asthma and other illnesses went up to the hills to gasp fresh air in Davos, St Moritz, Verbier, Gstaad etc. The farmers and hoteliers brought necessities for the hotel from the valley down below during rainy or snowy days, At that time, everyone knew everyone. It was more a family hospitality.

During the start of the hotel industry in France, at the beginning of the 15th century, the law required that hotels keep a register. English law also introduced rules for inns at that time. At the same time, around 1500 thermal spas were developed at Carlsbad and Marienbad.

During this epoch, more than 600 inns were registered in England. Their architecture often consisted of a paved interior court with access through an arched porch. The bedrooms were situated on the two sides of the courtyard, the kitchen and the public rooms at the front, and the stables and storehouses at the back. The first guide books for travellers were published in France during this period.

An embryonic hotel industry began to develop in Europe. Distinctive signs were hung outside establishments renowned for their refined cuisine.

In Paris in the time of Louis XIV, the Place Vendôme offered the first example of a multiple-use architectural complex, where the classical façades accommodated boutiques, offices, apartments and also hotels.

In the 19th century, hotels took over the town -The industrial revolution, which started in the 1760s, facilitated the construction of hotels everywhere, in mainland Europe, in England, USA and Switzerland.

In Japan, ryokan guest houses sprang up. In India, the government-run dak bungalows provided reliable accommodation for travellers. The Tremont House in Boston was the first deluxe hotel in a city centre. It offered inside toilets, locks on the doors and an 'à la carte' menu.

In 1822, in Venice, a certain gentleman named Giuseppe Dal Niel transformed an old palace into a hotel and gave it his name, 'Le Danieli'. As trains began to replace horse-drawn transport, highway inns for stage coaches started to decline.

During this period, the Shepheard's Hotel in Cairo was founded, the result of a complete transformation of an ancient city-center harem.

L'Hôtel des Bergues was built in the spring of 1834 on the shore of the Lake of Geneva. One of its founders, Guillaume Henri Dufour, became a famous Swiss general.

In 1840, l'Hôtel des Trois Couronnes was established in Vevey, Switzerland and the Baur au Lac in Zurich.

The 'Bayerischer Hof' was built in Munich in 1841, followed by the 'Vier Jahreszeiten' in 1852. These two famous establishments were completely renovated after the Second World War.

The Fifth Avenue Hotel in New York City was the first in that period to provide lifts for its guests. 1869 saw the inauguration, near Cairo, of the Mena House, an oasis of calm and luxury, at the foot of the famous pyramids of Cheops, Chephren and Mikerinos.

In 1870, the Palmer House Hotel in Chicago was the grandest of all hotels. Its structure, the first of its kind, was fire-resistant.

In 1873, the Palais de Württemberg in Vienna was transformed into a superb luxury residence for the notables of the epoch, and was known as l'Hôtel Impérial. Kings and queens became regular visitors to what was without doubt the finest example of the refined architecture of the Ring Strasse in Vienna. It is said that Richard Wagner directed the first productions of 'Tannhäuser' and 'Lohengrin' there. Two years later in 1875, the Grand Hotel Europe opened its doors in St Petersburg. This prestigious place is where Tchaikovsky spent his honeymoon and where Shostakovich played a sonata for Prokofiev in his suite.

The first school for hoteliers was founded in Lausanne, Switzerland in 1890 by J. Tschumi, Director of the Beau Rivage in Lausanne, and A.R. Armleder, the 'father' of the Richemond in Genève.

The Swiss hotelier Caspar Badrutt opened the famous Palace de St. Moritz in 1896. In 1898, César Ritz, from the Valais in Switzerland, who became, to quote the famous phrase of King Edward VII, the 'king of hoteliers and hotelier to kings', opened the hotel, which bears his famous name in the Place Vendôme in Paris.

The 20th century: the age of prosperity -The early years of the 20th century were rich in new hotels, which rapidly became prestigious.

Edouard Niiermans, the 'architect of palaces', transformed the Villa 'Eugenie', the summer residence of the Emperor Napoléon III and his wife Eugénie de Montijo, in 1900. In 1905, he built l'Hôtel du Palais in Biarritz. In 1913, his 'Négresco' was opened in Nice, in the presence of seven kings!

In Madrid, King Alphonse XIII was anxious that the capital should have a luxurious and prestigious hotel, and as a result, the Ritz was inaugurated in 1910. Seville paid its own homage to the king by opening a splendid establishment, constructed by the architect José Espiau, the Alphonso XIII. Not to be outdone, Barcelona inaugurated its own Ritz in 1919. This was equipped with an unheard-of luxury at that time, bathrooms with hot as well as cold water!

We could also cite, among many other hotels built in the same period, the Ritz and Savoy in London, the Beau Rivage Palace in Lausanne, le Négresco in Nice, the Plaza in New York, the Métropole in Brussels, the Plaza-Athenée and l'Hôtel de Crillon in Paris, the Taj Mahal in Bombay and so on. The latter was renovated in 1972 by the Inter-Continental chain.

The prosperous 1920s saw a veritable boom in the hotel industry. Numerous hotels were established in this decade. In 1923, the architects Marchisio and Prost constructed a hotel in some wonderful gardens in the heart of Marrakech in Morocco, and for decades it was considered the most beautiful hotel in the world: La Mamounia.

Winston Churchill helped to forge its reputation by becoming a frequent guest.

Hotels were built not only in cities, but also in the mountains. The first ski resorts in Switzerland (St-Moritz, Gstaad, Montana, etc.) welcomed tourists (often English ones) to some very comfortable establishments.

The worldwide depression, which followed in 1929 did not prevent the construction of the famous Waldorf Astoria in New York. This was the greatest hotel edifice of those troubled times.

After the war, the fifties saw the second boom in the hotel industry. The Club Méditerranée (G. Trigano) created the now famous, but then revolutionary concept of the club village. These years were also notable for the construction of the first casino hotels. This was also the time when the airline companies began to develop their own hotels.

In the 60s, new tourist resorts flourished around the Mediterranean. From Spain to Greece and from the Balearics to Yugoslavia, numerous city and beach hotels opened their doors to summer guests hungry for relaxation and a good dose of sunshine. Portugal and the Scandinavian countries soon followed their lead.

1970 saw the beginning of the construction of hotels for business people. This movement was supported by several factors. First of all, there was the will of the airline companies to extend their efforts in the domain of hotels.

Then there was the sudden prosperity of Middle Eastern countries due to black gold, which attracted business people from the entire world. This engendered an important business travel trend - not limited to this region alone - which initiated the development of hotels primarily designed for business people in Middle-Eastern cities like Dubai, Abu Dhabi, Riyadh and Jeddah, to mention only the most important.

Hotel chains, attentive to their customers' wishes, started to offer an increasingly varied range of services. Their rooms became more spacious and the cuisine more refined.

Gradually, too, various first-class hotels (among them former palaces and city center hotels),which had fallen into disrepair began systematic renovation programmes.

The end of the 70s, when China opened its doors to foreign tourists, also saw the first congresses of international hotel experts.

The third hotel industry boom -The third boom in the hotel industry began in 1980, marked by more inventive marketing and the development of hotels increasingly adapted to a particular type of clientele.

This trend prompted the construction of hotels near airports, hotels for conferences, health hotels, ski holiday hotels, holiday villages and marina hotels. The first Property Management Systems (Fidelio, Hogatex, etc.) appeared in the hospitality market.

In Istanbul in 1984, work began on the renovation and transformation of the prestigious sultans' residence into a hotel, the Ciragan Palace in Istanbul. The resulting hotel is no less prestigious than what the Ciragan Palace was. Managed by the Kempinski - a German hotel chain, it opened its 322 rooms to guests in 1991.

The first administrative hotel management systems, offering hotels greater independence from human resources, appeared in the market then. The hotel industry was becoming more and more competitive. Business travellers and retired people became important target customers.

In the 80s too, the Far East began to prepare itself to welcome both business people and the tourists who were beginning to discover the countries of the rising sun, such as China, South Korea, Thailand and Japan. The international chains (American for the most part) prepared expansion plans for Europe, the Middle and Far East, which were mainly aimed at congress participants and business people.

The 90s: technology started to make an impact -The early 90s were characterised by a recession in the hotel business, which was without doubt caused by reductions in multinationals' travel budgets and the growing crisis in the Gulf.

The Gulf War helped to create great insecurity for both individuals and businesses. 1991 was considered to be the black year of the hotel trade. It forced hoteliers to become more creative in finding ways of attracting guests (special programmes, offers for 'frequent travellers', high performance reservation systems) to emerge from the crisis with minimum damage.

For the first time, the environment and energy conservation played an important role in the marketing activities of numerous chains (thanks in part to the green movement) and even helped to win the loyalty of numerous clients while safeguarding assets at the same time.

Reservation systems became more efficient and offered the hotelier a new dimension in the creation of customer loyalty through the database. The records of each guest's individual history have helped create individualised marketing programmes and have enabled hotels to satisfy a guest's personal needs from the moment of his arrival.

Hotel Adlon Berlin is a legend reborn. From its opening in 1907, until it was destroyed in 1945, it was a symbol of Berlin, a lavish host for royalty, heads of government, stage and screen stars, and the greats of literature and science. Now, it has been rebuilt (1997) on its original site, the corner of Unter den Linden and Pariser Platz, facing the Brandenburg Gate. Outside, it is a virtual replica of the original; inside it is testimony to what smart hotel operators (in this case the Kempinski group) can accomplish with an investment of $260 million. The hotel's 337 rooms and suites are the ultimate in luxury. Interiors, designed by England's Ezra Attia and Sweden's Lars Malmquist, dazzle with marble, sandstone, stained glass, gold leaf, stuccowork, cherry wood panelling, and damask draperies. This hotel is today equipped with the most advanced technology with regards

to the Room Management System communicating with the
Property Management System.

Since 1992, the most important international chains have
been vying with each other in ever greater imaginative
feats related to the vital process of renovating their
establishments worldwide. Technology has started to take
its rightful place in hotel administration (simplification
of check-in and check-out procedures, global reservation
systems, marketing management etc.). In 1995, the first
Hotel Room Management System was launched at the
European level. It was linked to the most popular Property
Management Systems to make the front desk more efficient
and near to the guests.

Impact of technnology

At International Technology Forums, speakers unanimously,
underlined the impact of technology on hotel rooms.

Hotel chains have been searching for alliances and some
of them for example, Holiday Inn, Intercontinental Hotels
and Crown Plaza have merged to form Six Continents
hotel chain; Marriott absorbed Renaissance and Ramada
International; Sol Melia opened a new line of Boutique
hotels, Accor signed several joint ventures in the East and
the Far East, etc. Forte acquired Méridien to reinforce its
global position. Starwoods (Sheraton) absorbed the Italian
Ciga chain and Westin.

The main expansion zones for the hotel industry in 1994
remained in Asia (particularly China and India), the Middle
East (above all, the United Arab Emirates and Egypt) and
Latin America.

In Europe, hotel enterprises in the eastern countries (Russia, Croatia, Slovakia, etc.) decided to renovate dilapidated palaces built at the turn of the century. All the European capitals started to invest in preparations for the major event of this fin de siècle period, that is, the celebration of our entry into the third millennium.

The 4-star Hotel Millennium enjoying top level of Online Room Management System is situated at the best site in Opatija at the Mediterranean coast. Opatija in Croatia corresponds, in terms of reputation, to the level of St. Moritz in Switzerland.

Capitals throughout the world were busy developing the necessary infrastructure to welcome the millions of tourists for the celebration of this event.

Major hotel chains were drawing up development plans in almost all parts of Europe. These plans primarily involved the renovation of numerous prestigious hotels in both western and eastern European countries. Gradually, the great capitals of Europe have been endowed with hotels boasting three, four and five stars, offering quality services, innovative architecture, style, charm, and interior design (city Boutique hotels). Specialised hotels offered wellness programmes including health and beauty centers, personalised services and treatments, anti-stress, revitalising, regenerating programmes etc.

Extravaganza - In 1995, construction began in Dubai for one of the most ambitious and prestigious tourist complexes in the region, the Jumeirah Beach Hotels (Jumeirah Beach hotel, Burj Al Arab, etc.). These comprised of several establishments capable of satisfying the needs of average tourists, business people and those who could not afford real luxury. The talk then was of six- and seven-star hotels, a surprising designation, which was nevertheless perfectly justified by the luxury of the bedrooms and the facilities they offered, the impeccable service, the high degree of modern technology, as well as the beauty of the surroundings and the high-quality environment.

In 2004, another emirate, Abu Dhabi, was set to welcome the delegates of the Gulf Council Countries in the new Conference Palace Hotel (CPH). This superior construction has been specified 'to offer the most outstanding services with a challenging 9 star definition'... What will that be like?

Online in seconds, work surfing, communicate-everywhere... In 2003, travellers, mostly businessmen, carried their personal PC to make presentations, communicate with their office via e-mails, etc. One possibility offered to them today consists in the use of so-called Pad offering, in particular:

- Cable-free and universal access to the Internet or intranet, wherever you happen to be
- Brilliant colour touch screen
- Ready to go in seconds (instant on)
- Freedom in the selection of transmission standards by interchangeable PC cards
- Unlimited flexibility by open platform Windows CE 3.0
- Comprehensive office software package
- Virtual keyboard and handwriting recognition

For sure, new technologies are continuously offering innovative and more comfortable ways to the traveller.

Conclusion - Lodging facilities are no longer corresponding only to the definition: 'A lodging accommodation for travellers'. Nowadays, architects, designers, developers, engineers, managers, more and more are conscious that the taste of guests could be different, according to their wishes or needs. Hotel specialists permanently analyse new trends, define better criteria, present modern standards in order to improve quality of life in hotels. In the third millennium, the permanent competitive hospitality market of suppliers is definitely more and more able, combining 'savoir faire' and the good use of technology to offer their guests an 'a la carte' environment.

But in 1930, depression in the hotel industry was noticed. It felt that the hotel industry would never recover, but the outbreak of the World War brought a tremendous upsurge. Up until the 50s, this prosperity continued and operation started becoming prominent in this period. Later on, it was felt by the individual owners that the international chain operation would help in terms of expensive technology and marketing thrust, what they themselves could not provide. So, there was no way out for the individual owners except to merge with large international establishments such as Sheraton, Hilton, Holiday Inn etc. These international chains provided the following to the individual owners – Partner, Franchise or Management contract.

Let's fast forward a bit. Marketing firms suddenly popped up everywhere, studying customers' wants and needs and creating commercials and large billboards with captivating slogans. Now that worked quite well, and we still use billboards to attract roadside travellers today. Hotels branched out into corporate brands, and suddenly we had an economy of branded properties (Motel 6) drive-in, mid-tier properties (Hampton Inn and Holiday Inn) and even resort-type properties (Doubletree and Hilton). Catchy jingles and emotionally targeted commercials that showcased laughing families in hotel rooms were produced to bring in customers. Competition was fierce, and the need to incorporate new marketing strategies was stronger than ever.

Customers had more options for where to stay and got greedy for more amenities. Hotel owners strived to create the best guest experience to compete with branded chains at the lowest possible price. Marketing campaigns and reward programmes became huge and came with a hefty price tag. 'Stay two nights and get one night free', or 'double reward points for two consecutive stays' – whatever it took to bring in customers.

Economic booms were on the rise, hotels popped up everywhere and rooms filled. That was when the online travel agencies (OTAs) came in – the proverbial elephant in the marketing room. Companies like Priceline, Expedia and Booking.com were booking rooms for us, but hotels were paying high fees. When the economy started suffering, those fees felt magnified. Today, technology is a critical factor in the effort to grow revenue while managing rising costs. Hotels now are using a wide range of data analytics to set rates and connect with customers in an effort to gain repeat business. The biggest trend we see today is the need to stray away from OTAs as the primary booking source and lead customers toward direct booking.

Hoteliers today are looking to established web designers to create custom websites that are feature-rich and integrate direct-booking channels to avoid the pricey OTA fees. Custom websites award customers with professional photography, links to restaurants and entertainment, direct customer reviews and even virtual tours. Best of all, guests can book rooms directly from the hotels and save money by receiving the best rates possible; the hotels save money as well by avoiding commission fees. Content is the key, and hotel owners want to provide guests with information that is not only relatable but that uses words and phrases to paint the customer a panoramic picture that they will want to read more about and then book.

Millennials have become the fastest growing segment in the hospitality industry. This customer segment is turning toward technology to get that 'unique and novel' hotel experience. Be assured that if a stay is not anything short of spectacular, then Facebook, Twitter and Instagram will know immediately. This is where social media marketing comes into play. It's not enough to have a custom website, but it has to be linked to all social media outlets and constantly monitored and updated to reach the widest range of customers in today's market.

Marketing evolution is inevitable, but it takes a major change in the operating climate for hotel owners to recognise the need for change. Hospitality organisations and experienced Marketing Revenue Managers constantly organise workshops to keep owners aware and educated on the growing technological trends. And owners are also attending or sending staff to conferences to see how the market is changing.

So what can we expect in the years to come? More, more and more. More mobile bookings, more targeted content, more personalised emails, more video marketing and more educational conferences. And we can expect technology to be in the forefront of all these trends.

Customisation in a hotel can start before the potential guests even become guests. Different advertisements or content focusing on different aspects of your hotel should be targeted at different people depending on their preferences as they have expressed online. Once they arrive, personalisation could be achieved by recommending specific leisure activities depending on each guest's personality and taste. Another way would be remembering returning guests' personal information and tastes (regarding meals, for example).

Automated emails asking for feedback after a stay is a good way to record customers' preferences, as well as to know how your hotel can improve.

Smartphones and tablets already control almost all aspects of our lives—from business to travel, grocery shopping to medical appointments. Self-service claims have become the present age currency. As a result, when it comes to hotel accommodations, guests want to experience the same self-service alternatives. This article is from Trilyo, which provides self-service hospitality solutions like room bookings, check-ins and check-outs, and personalised payments. We will take a look at how automation is becoming a part of the hospitality industry and how it is improving the guest experience.

Digital Room Keys

The new era of hotel entry is keyless, cardless and is re-defining the standards of guest experience. As in the case of 17 Marriott Hotels, the Marriott Mobile App is now the room key for guests enabling them to skip the front desk and check-in to gain access to their room and other hotel services. This automation frees up hotel staff, allowing them to engage with guests and provide an exceptional experience for them. Furthermore, it helps the hotel in branding and acquiring a loyal customer base. However, OTAs such as Expedia might give hotels a run for their money as they are coming up with a keyless-entry feature on their own mobile-booking apps!

Guestroom Automation

The Shangri-la Hotel in Abu Dhabi houses 214 rooms and has successfully implemented a state-of-the-art Guest Automation System. When the hotel reservation system switches the status of a room from 'Vacant' to 'Occupied', the central station adjusts the room temperature to an ideal level as guests head towards their room. The system also provides valuable operational data such as staff response to the guest call, energy saving data, room occupancy status etc., thus reducing manual errors by the hotel staff significantly.

Artificial Intelligence

Hotels are now using AI to create unique and memorable customer experiences in combination with automated room features. For instance, when a room is programmed by the guest to 'wakeup' during the morning hours, AI could trigger automated features such as the drapes opening and turning on a preferred news or radio station.

Currently the Al Ain Rotana in UAE, which houses 90 guest rooms, provides guests with in-room personalisation as well. Each room consists of a smart bedside console from where the guest can operate all the lights in the room, switch the air-conditioning on or off, and adjust and view the temperature in the room as part of the Guest Automation System.

AI could also be used, in the form of push marketing offers or chatbots, to remind hotel guests to grab a meal or drink from the onsite bar and restaurant, to schedule a room cleaning service, or to add a spa service to their stay.

Improving Environmental Impact

Utility costs are approx. 6% of the total cost. Energy costs are on the rise and so is environmental consciousness, so hoteliers must shift towards sustainable practices, and the best way to start is with the guest rooms. Lights and air conditioning can be shut off based on guest activity and room occupancy. For example, if a guest is on the balcony, the sensors in the other room spaces 'notice' and will switch to standby mode. Plus, guests enjoy a great welcome experience when the welcome lights turn on upon arrival, then sensors switch them off automatically when the main lights come on.

Mobile Concierge Services

As the consumer tendency shifts toward text messages and voice chats over phone calls or in-person communication, mobile concierge services will become more in demand. The Marriott Mobil App already offers this with its feature called 'Ask Anything'. It is a round-the-clock concierge service that attends to beyond basic requests like ordering bath and bed linens, room-cleaning services or just a simple 'Where is the best place to go out tonight?' It can also connect guests directly to a staff member, bypassing the phone or a visit at the front desk.

Guest Reviews

Hotels often shy away from confronting their guests to ask for reviews. Automated Feedback Systems send pre-scheduled emails to recently checked-out guests. As a result, staff time and effort are greatly reduced as customers can sit back and write about their stay on their way to the airport without being bothered by front desk staff.

Voice Command Technology

More hotels are offering in-room voice command technology. When placed by the bedside console and equipped to understand voice commands, this personal assistant can offer many of the same amenities as a concierge. It could also be used to control every aspect of lighting, temperature and the audio-visual components of a hotel room. Plus, it could be seamlessly integrated with in-house offers and even greet your guests with a 'Good morning!' when they wake up.

LIVING AT HOME AND ABROAD

Here's a little history of my country- Switzerland.

In my early childhood, the milkman would stop by our house and every other house every morning, and put butter, eggs and fill our stainless steel container with milk (if required) in our letter box and we would pay the bill at the end of each week.

For bread, we had to go to a special bakery shop nearby, and for meat and other grocery items, we had to visit a nearby special shop.

Today, the whole process of buying items has changed to large non-personal shopping malls, and a big amount via online purchase.

We did not take a bus to school but walked for approx. 2 km each way (through rain, snow or sun).

At the end of the war, Swiss politics and neutrality were internationally compromised because Switzerland had maintained relations with Nazi Germany until its demise.

The Soviet Union only reluctantly accorded diplomatic recognition to Switzerland, which had been a herald of anticommunism in the interwar period.

In a 1946 agreement, the Western Allies, especially the United States, compelled Switzerland to compensate the looted western European central banks, requiring the payment of some 250 million Swiss francs.

Because Switzerland would have received no special recognition of its neutrality, the Council decided not to join the <u>United Nations</u> (UN), which nonetheless occupied offices in <u>Geneva</u>.

Joining the <u>North Atlantic Treaty Organization</u> (NATO), the U.S.-led western alliance was never a serious option for a <u>country</u> that believed armed neutrality had been the best defence against <u>Nazism</u> and would also save the country from <u>communism</u>.

The <u>Cold War</u> allowed Switzerland to again become a respectable member of the international community. Neutrality enabled it to play a mediating role between the two antagonistic camps, but, as a capitalist democracy with a strong citizens army, it was a tacit member of the noncommunist world and one of its key defenders. An interesting and complicated mixture of neutrality, isolationism, solidarity, anticommunism, and militarism became the common, often complacent ideology of most Swiss, be they bourgeois or socialist.

Switzerland's strong economy attracted many <u>immigrants,</u> first from <u>Italy</u> and <u>Spain</u> and after 1980, from Yugoslavia and <u>Turkey</u>.

Switzerland has also kept a conservative approach to several other issues. For example, <u>women</u> were enfranchised on the national level only in 1971, and in the canton of <u>Appenzell,</u> they had to wait until 1990 for full <u>voting rights</u>.

Relatively late, in 1981, an equal rights amendment was added to the <u>constitution,</u> and in 1985, the rather patriarchal <u>marriage law</u> was amended.

Another problem that had lasted for decades was resolved pragmatically in 1978, when a national referendum authorised Jura, a French-speaking Catholic area of the Protestant canton of Bern, to form its own canton.

Recent developments

In the 1990s, Switzerland was one of the world's wealthiest and most prosperous countries, and neutrality, still the country's official doctrine, became much more complicated. In 1986 some three-fourths of voters rejected entry into the UN, despite the endorsement of membership by most mainstream politicians. Though opposed to joining the association, Switzerland sided with the UN against Iraq's invasion of Kuwait during the Persian Gulf War (1990–91).

In a later referendum in 2002, a very small majority approved entry into the UN. Yet, the changed proportions showed that decisive and seemingly contradictory changes occurred in a few years. In 1989 for example, some one-third of voters endorsed a referendum proposing the abolition of the Swiss army, which had been considered the untouchable backbone of Swiss sovereignty. On the other hand, in 1992, Swiss voters narrowly turned down membership in a European Economic Area that comprised of the European Union (EU) and European Free Trade Association (EFTA). Because most EFTA members had joined the EU, Switzerland was politically isolated within Europe at the beginning of the 21st century. However, it maintained strong bilateral economic ties with the EU, which was by far its largest trading partner.

In 2008, Switzerland acceded to the Schengen Agreement, a European convention aimed at reducing international border controls between member countries. While there was significant popular opposition to joining the Schengen area, proponents cited the benefits of decreased congestion at border checkpoints and access to the Schengen Information System (SIS), a database containing information about persons and goods traversing the Schengen zone. Switzerland's relationship with the EU was further complicated in February 2014, when Swiss voters approved a referendum that imposed quotas on immigration. The result directly challenged a number of existing bilateral agreements and called into question Switzerland's continued presence in the Schengen area.

At the end of the 20th century, growing doubts about Switzerland's past and future had emerged.

Many Swiss questioned the country's traditional 'bunker mentality' in a Europe at peace and with open borders. Particularly troubling for Switzerland was an international debate during the 1990s about 'dormant accounts'—assets left by Jews in Swiss banks during the Nazi era but never returned—a controversy that challenged Switzerland's image of itself and resulted in a settlement between two large commercial banks and Jewish plaintiffs in which the banks agreed to pay international Jewish organisations two billion Swiss francs (about $1.25 billion).

Financial officials estimated that hundreds of millions of dollars in dormant assets remained unclaimed in Swiss banks in the early 21st century. Efforts to disburse those funds were fueled, at least in part, by foreign governments that sought to compel Swiss banks to reveal the identities of their account holders for tax purposes.

Switzerland calmly weathered the crisis that had rocked the euro zone in the 2010s, and that stability drew increased immigration from its EU neighbours. The terms of the 2014 referendum were significantly softened in December 2016, so as not to jeopardise bilateral trade agreements with the EU, and the right of free movement was finally extended to Croatian citizens.

In September 2017, a massive pension reform package was narrowly rejected by voters. The measure, which would have stabilised the country's old-age social security scheme with an increase to the value-added tax, was the most comprehensive attempt in a generation to address the challenge of supporting Switzerland's ageing population.

Switzerland, which has had one of the most successful national histories in Europe, faces unique problems in a time of peace and prosperity. Its archaic aspects—such as the autonomous communes that form the basis of Swiss citizenship—reflect political continuity that have endured, despite having gone through frequent dramatic social changes. For a long time, the Swiss have attributed their good fortune to their own virtues, especially democratic federalism, political moderation and stability, neutrality, humanitarianism, valour, and diligence. However, Swiss exceptionalism appears more and more questionable. Moreover, the controversies over Switzerland's historical role have challenged its self-image as an island of virtue.

Yet, for people of diverse cultures and languages, political uniqueness has largely constituted its national identity. Can this country based on a sense of otherness survive in its present form, or will its different linguistic regions join their big neighbours on linguistic grounds if Switzerland should further renounce its sovereignty and join the EU?

Today in 2020, the population of Switzerland is approximately 8.3 million inclusive of approximately 1 million refugees from Syria, Lebanon, Libya etc. In 2015, Germany started accepting millions of refugees from the mentioned countries and distributed them to the various European countries. Switzerland had to take in some of these refugees or we would be isolated in our trade agreement.

My time in Malaysia - 1981 to 1983, 1993 to 1999 and 2015

During my time in Malaysia, Tun Dr. Mohamad Mahathir was the PM from 1981 till 2003 and from 2018 till 2020.

Majority of the population were and still are Muslims, followed by the Chinese and Indian communities, which together, form a very colorful mix with some occasional disagreements.

Malaysia is located on a strategic sea-lane that exposes it to global trade and various cultures. Strictly, the name 'Malaysia' is a modern concept, created in the second half of the 20th century. However, contemporary Malaysia regards the entire history of Malaya and Borneo, spanning thousands of years back to prehistoric times.

Although Muslims had passed through the Malay Peninsular as early as the 10th century, it was not until the 14th century that Islam first firmly established itself.

The adoption of Islam in the 14th century saw the rise of several sultanates, the most prominent were the Sultanate of Malacca and the Sultanate of Brunei. Islam has a profound influence on the Malay people until today.

The Portuguese were the first European colonial powers to establish themselves on the Malay Peninsular and Southeast Asia, capturing Malacca in 1511. This was followed by the Dutch in 1641. However, it was the English who, after initially establishing bases in Kuching, Penang and Singapore, ultimately secured their hegemony across the territory that is now Malaysia.

The Japanese invasion during World War 2 ended the British rule in Malaya. After the Japanese surrendered from Malaya as a result of being defeated by the Allies, the Malayan Union was established in 1946 by the British administration but following opposition by the ethnic Malays, the union was reorganised as the Federation of Malaya in 1948 as a protectorate state until 1957.

Singapore and Brunei are independent states today. Brunei is very rich in oil reserves whereas Singapore is a financial hub in Asia.

I still remember when I first visited KL, there was a race track in the heart of the city and it had to give way to the KLCC Twin Towers, which is now the centre of the city. During this time also, many new buildings came up in Kuala Lumpur and other areas. International Hotel chains joined the area. Malaysia started to become an international hub.

The Asian financial crisis started in Thailand on 2 July 1997, with the financial collapse of the Thai baht. This happened after the Thai government was forced to float the baht due to a lack of foreign currency to support its currency which was pegged to the US dollar. At the time, Thailand had acquired a burden of foreign debts. As the crisis spread, most of Southeast Asia and Japan saw slumping currencies, devalued stock markets and other asset prices, and a precipitous rise in private departments.

Indonesia, Korea and Thailand were the countries most affected by the crisis. Hong Kong, Laos, Malaysia and the Philippines were also hurt by the slump.

Brunei, Mainland China, Singapore, Taiwan and Vietnam were less affected, although all suffered from a loss of demand and confidence throughout the region. Japan was also affected, though less significantly.

My project with some local, Taiwanese and Hong Kong investors in Johor was called off and I had to look for a new assignment. I took up a hotel consultancy job in Klang, a large port area, which was one hour drive from Kuala Lumpur city.

I helped a local Chinese hotel owner build his 250-room, 4-star hotel, known as the 'Gold Course'. After completion of the construction, we hired a General Manager to continue as I applied with Holiday Inn KL to be their Training Manager. However, this job did not materialise as the Asian Crisis went deeper and deeper and they could not afford a foreigner.

Luckily, I bought an apartment in the heart of KL where I am staying until today. (The monthly maintenance fee of the building and the service charge were low so I was able to stay longer. However my work permit was at stake.)

All foreign labourers in all categories were asked to go for a cool off period of 6 months till the Asian crisis had a better footing. My last effort was to open a small *nasi lemak* stall in the city centre so that I could survive and pay some 3 employees their salary. Unfortunately, my permit came to an end.

1997–2000

During the Asian financial crisis, Malaysia faced a large depreciation of the ringgit and massive capital flight, even though it raised domestic interest rates. To stem this outflow and depreciation, the government fixed the value of the ringgit at RM3.8 to US$1 to manage the impossible trinity problem. This allowed it to lower interest rates to stimulate the economy without worrying about capital flight or currency volatility. When the economy started to recover in 1999, capital and currency controls were gradually relaxed and finally removed. In February of 1999, the one-year moratorium on repatriation of profits from share sale was replaced by a 10 percent exit levy on the sale proceeds on a graduated scale.

2001–2005

From 2001 to 2005, the government relaxed capital controls but still maintained the pegged ringgit. But at the same time, it also resorted to monetary instruments, via sterilisation and its reverse, to smoothen out the effects of capital flows. In 2001, the exit levy was abolished altogether. Residents were gradually allowed to operate foreign currency accounts and to invest abroad. As the economy recovered, capital began to flow back into the country. In 2003, net portfolio investment was a positive RM4.2 billion, up from a negative RM6.5 billion a year earlier. It surged to RM33 billion in 2004.

From 2005 onwards, the exchange rate and capital flow policies became almost fully liberalised. Capital controls were removed and the pegged ringgit was lifted in July 2005 and changed to a managed-float system. But the ringgit remained non-internationalised, that is, there were limits to non-residents borrowing in the local currency.

Sharm El Sheikh, Egypt on the Red Sea

Before 1967, Sharm El Sheikh was a little more than an occasional base of operations for local fishermen; the nearest permanent settlement was in Nabk, north of Ras El Nasrani ('The Tiran Straits'). Commercial development of the area began during the Israeli presence in the area. The Israelis built the town of Ofira overlooking Sharm El Maya Bay and the Nesima area, and opened the first tourist-oriented establishments in the area 6 km north at Naama Bay. These included a marina hotel on the southern side of the bay, a nature field school on the northern side, diving clubs, a now well-known promenade, and the Naama Bay Hotel. The site off the shore gun emplacements at Ras Nasrani, opposite Tiran Island, is now a diving area.

After Sinai was restored to Egypt in 1982, the Egyptian government embarked on an initiative to encourage continued development of the city. Foreign investors – some of whom had discovered the potential of the locality during the Israeli occupation – contributed to a spate of building projects. Environmental zoning laws currently limit the height of buildings in Sharm El Sheikh so as to avoid obscuring the natural beauty of the surroundings.

In July 2005, the resort Sharm el Sheikh was hit by a terrorist attack, which were perpetrated by an extremist Islamite organisation and aimed at Egypt's tourist industry. A total of 88 people were killed, the majority of them Egyptians, and over 200 were wounded by the attack, making it the deadliest terrorist action in the country's history (exceeding the Luxor attack of 1997). This was for any GM, a nightmare, as in front of our hotel alone, 35 persons were killed. A suicide bomber was trying to drive into our hotel, the Ghazala and the Moevenpick in Naama Bay. We had extensive damages to the hotel front. The boutiques and 2 restaurants, which faced the old market were also damaged. Fortunately, we had no casualties in the hotel. The guests, mostly foreigners, were in the room and the security guard at the front had left his station to look for the toilet during the time of the attack.

The tourists were evacuated within 48 hours and we stood there with our brooms and shovels to clear the mess.

In October the same year (3 months later), occupancy picked up again as tourists were forgetful and needed to escape from the cold European weather.

The city has played host to a number of important Middle Eastern peace conferences, including the 4 September 1999 agreement to restore Palestinian self-rule over the Gaza strip. A second summit was held at Sharm on 17 October 2000 following the outbreak of the second Palestinian intifada, but it failed to end the violence.

A summit was held in the city on 3 August 2005 on developments in the Arab world, addressing issues such as the situation in the Arab-Israeli conflict. Again in 2007, an important ministerial meeting took place in Sharm, where dignitaries discussed Iraqi reconstruction. The World

Economic Forum on the Middle East was also hosted by Sharm el-Sheikh in 2006 and 2008.

Amidst the 2011 Egyptian protest, President Hosni Mubarak went to Sharm El Sheikh and resigned in February 2011. After this reign of dictatorship, 2 following presidents lasted only 3 years till the uprising of the military and until today it is run by General al-Sisi.

As you read correctly in 2005, we had some terrorist intruders in Sharm El Sheikh and it was time for me to go back to Asia. Moevenpick Hotels-Resorts with the headquarters in Zurich, offered me a job in Tunisia or in Aqaba (Jordan). Having spent 7 years in Egypt, I declined the offer and accepted the job in Moevenpick Resort & Spa Karon Beach Phuket. After spending 35 years in Asia, I guess it was the right choice to go back to the Land of Smiles.

The Philippines

Manila, the capital city of the Philippines, is the centre of the country's economic, political, social, and cultural activity. It is located on the island of Luzon and spreads along the eastern shore of Manila Bay at the mouth of the Pasig River.

Within the area of Metropolitan Manila, public transportation is provided principally by buses, jeepneys (small buses built on the chassis of jeeps) and taxis. Traffic congestion is serious, especially at the bridges during the morning and evening rush hours. Adjacent towns serve as dormitory suburbs, and many people commute to the city, adding to the traffic problem. Bus services operate routes to northern and southern Luzon.

The Philippines spreads over 7000 Islands. While some are sparsely occupied, others have more inhabitants. Some can be reached by boats only and others by small planes.

When things became bad in Manila, the government imposed a complete lockdown especially during the evening from 8 pm to 8 am the following day, so people could not gather and have assemblies.

The local currency was peso. I earned USD850 nett per month, lived in a hotel room on the same floor as all other expats. All meals were provided by the hotel. We also had a 50% discount on food and beverage items if we wished to invite friends for meals.

The US had a long contract with the Philippines and established a military base in case of any wars with the surrounding countries, with special attention given to China.

The upscale and slums

The very rich Filipinos lived in Dasmarinas or very close to all other luxury hotels. The housing area was gated with heavy security. The sad parts are the slum areas in the main capital. Slums can be found in many communities, located in all the cities and municipalities of Metro Manila.

These slum communities are located on vacant lands that are both private and government-owned. Usually they are located along rivers and creeks, in garbage dumps, along railroad tracks, under bridges, and beside factories and other industrial establishments. Slums located next to mansions in affluent residential areas are not uncommon.

Power of the church

Since the colonial period, Catholicism has been the cornerstone of Filipino identity for millions in the Philippines. Catholicism spread rapidly during the early years of Spanish colonialism, in part due to a lack of otherwise centralised religious institutions, other than Islam in the south, which might have challenged it. Its close associations with Filipino identity have placed the Catholic Church at the heart of nationalism, social justice, and other movements, while at the same time has been associated with power, elitism, and exploitation at various points in its history.

While initially popular, Marcos' tenure is remembered as a dark period of deep corruption, violence, chaos, and repression of Filipino society. During this period, the church played various roles. While most priests were largely apolitical and many were afraid of being labeled as 'subversives', thus subject to arrest and abuse, many priests and nuns actively opposed Marcos, some even taking up arms against the state. Marcos initially attempted to coopt the political power of the church, but quickly became suspicious and turned against it.

The Marcos-Aquino Saga

President Ferdinand Marcos has been blamed again for the assassination of former Senator Benigno Aquino in 1983, which paved the way for a people-backed military mutiny, which forced out the former dictator and propped to power Corazon Aquino to the presidency in 1986, a local paper said.

After the term of Marcos, when Aquino became president in 1986 (after running versus Marcos in the snap polls), a mistrial at the Sandiganbyan was declared.

When her son Benigno Jr. became president in the 2010 polls, he did not formally blame Marcos and the Cojuangco relative for the death of his father.

The death of the elder Aquino sparked a strong anti-Marcos sentiment that culminated in the people-backed military mutiny in 1986. Fortunately, we do not have such corruption and wild wild west stories back home in Switzerland.

Thailand

Known worldwide for its charming locals, majestic lime stone cliffs and picture-postcard beaches and coastlines, Thailand is also home to an array of funny things, quirky idiosyncrasies and enchanting peculiarities. Odd and bizarre in Thailand seem to be measured by a unique yardstick altogether and the country is full of surprising oddities.

The Land of the Free

The name Thailand in the Thai language is Prathet Thai, which directly translates to 'Land of the Free'. It seems pretty apt then that this country is the sole country in the whole of South-East Asia to never have been colonised by any European nation. Considering that only very few countries in the world have managed to escape European rule, this in itself is a huge accomplishment.

A festival not for the fainthearted

Continuing along the theme of bizarre and weird festivals, the Phuket Vegetarian Festival is held every year in the month of October and despite what the name suggests, is a rather grisly affair. A key feature of this festival is the people who get involved in very gory self-mutilation and parade in trance-like states in an attempt to purify their souls. Along with the self-mutilation of piercing their faces and body parts with strange and everyday objects, the locals walk barefoot across hot coals and abstain from eating meat for the ninth lunar month of the Chinese calendar, with the belief that they will be rewarded with excellent health and peace of mind. This grotesque and gory festival is not for the squeamish, the woozy or the fainthearted.

Royalty rules

In Thailand, paying respect to the royal family is a very serious matter. The royal family is adored and deeply respected by its citizens and it is strictly against the law to criticise any member of the monarchy. The country has the lèse majesté law, which means that any disrespectful acts that are performed toward the king, queen or royal heirs are punished with imprisonment for treason. The popular Hollywood film, 'The King and I' was even banned from Thai cinemas as it was deemed to be derogatory to the king. Mother's and Father's Day in Thailand are also celebrations for the king and queen rather than for one's own mother and father and is celebrated nationwide by the Thai people. Lastly, in the capital of Bangkok, the overhead walkways and the monorail will simply come to a complete halt if any royal personage is passing beneath the platform.

This is because no layman should ever pass above the head of royalty.

Every man a Buddhist monk

In the past, all Thai young men under the age of twenty, of all social rankings, including princes and kings, became Buddhist monks for at least a short amount of time in their lifetime. Although it was never a national requirement, if from a Buddhist family, it was almost always done. Obtaining monkhood is considered to be a very blessed event and by dedicating a portion of one's life to Buddhism, it is believed that good karma will be bestowed upon the man's family. Today there are far fewer Buddhist men who observe the practice of monkhood.

No head-touching

It is considered disrespectful to touch anyone on their head, even a child's. In Thai culture, the head is considered to be the most important part of the body. As a result, no one should ever touch the head of another person. As a sign of respect and acknowledgment, Thais often try to keep their heads lower than the head of anyone older than themselves or anyone in a higher position. On the opposite end of the body, the feet are considered lowly as they are symbols of attachment to the ground or earth, which is deemed to be a cause of human suffering and struggle. For this reason, feet should always be tucked under one's body and if sitting down, one's feet must not point toward another person or any statue in a temple.

Venice of the East

Thailand was once referred to as 'Venice of the East'.

This was due to the many original buildings that were built on stilts over the Chao Phraya River as well as the many meandering canals that were a significant factor in Bangkok's trading activities. Although there are still a fair number of pretty canals in the capital for tourists and locals to enjoy boat rides along, due to the fact that Bangkok grew larger in time, the majority of canals were filled and paved and have become streets and pavements today.

Longest reigning monarch

King Bhumibol Adulyade reigned from 1946, and at the time of his death in 2017, was the world's longest-reigning head of state and the longest-reigning monarch in all of Thai history.

Thailand shares its borders with four different countries, namely Myanmar, Laos, Cambodia and Malaysia. And lastly, Thailand's most exported crop? Rice, of course! Followed by orchids, I think.

Nepal – Kathmandu

Nepal's largest city and its capital, Kathmandu, attracts all kinds of people like students, travellers, job-seekers, and entrepreneurs. They arrive here to study, work or do business, but most never leave the city, which is now home to an estimated 3 million people. I, like many Nepalis, came to Kathmandu for education in the early 1990s and since then have been a resident and even an admirer. Despite its many flaws, I have grown attached to Kathmandu, whose deep-rooted traditional heritage sits comfortably alongside its modernity.

Kathmandu is also the first stop for international visitors who come to experience Nepal. The city and its people will welcome you with open arms—but it may also overwhelm you.

First, make it out of the airport

Nepal's only international airport, serving Kathmandu, is a picture of chaos. The airport receives more passengers than it can handle. Though most foreigners are eligible for an on-arrival visa, it's better to apply in advance at an embassy, which could save some time when you arrive. Bring a few hundred U.S. dollars with you to change into Nepali rupees. And don't forget to fill out the immigration form *before* you land, so you can join the long lines sooner. Every minute helps you get out of the airport sooner.

Don't expect to see the Himalayas

Eight of the world's 10 tallest Himalayan peaks are in Nepal. You can see snow-capped mountains from Kathmandu, which lies in a bowl-shaped valley in central Nepal. But for the mesmerising view of the towering Himalayas, you will have to visit either in autumn (October and November) or in spring (April and May).

A mask is a must

Dust from road-widening projects, post-quake reconstruction, emissions from brick factories near the city, and of course, the smoke-belching vehicles that stay on the roads thanks to lax enforcement of regulations, have all contributed to the city's growing air pollution. Last year, the authorities also declared the tourist district of Thamel and inner parts of the city a vehicle-free zone, meaning cars, trucks, and mini-buses are not allowed to drive. While these efforts have had some impact, the best protection against pollution is a mask.

Travel wisely

Getting around Kathmandu can be daunting. The city doesn't have an efficient mass-transit system, and to the uninitiated, the traffic looks chaotic: drivers don't follow traffic rules, buses stop in the middle of the road, and bus passengers are crammed into every spare inch. There aren't too many choices. You will have to hop onto an overcrowded minibus or flag an overcharging taxi. If you do the latter, you should insist that the driver runs the meter, and if the driver refuses, don't be afraid to haggle. For locals, the cabbies normally charge 100 rupees per kilometre, but they may try to bump that up for foreigners. Once you know the distance, try to negotiate the fare.

Avoid the monsoon period

During monsoon, roads are waterlogged because they lack adequate sewage systems, vehicles splash muddy water on you, and even your umbrella may be of no match for the downpour. The running joke every monsoon in Kathmandu is that you can row a boat in its flooded streets. But the season also has its share of delights. The rain dripping off the eaves of your guesthouse or hotel, the emerald-green vista that emerges after the rain, and the occasional rainbow are a sight to behold.

PANDEMIC, RETIREMENT AND MOVING ON

On 31st December 2019, the World Health Organization (WHO) announced that China reports of a previously-unknown virus behind a number of pneumonia cases in Wuhan, the city that is located in Eastern China with a population of over 11 million.

What started as an epidemic mainly limited to China has now become a truly global pandemic. There have now been over 3,200,000 confirmed cases and 300,000 deaths. The Chinese government responded to the initial outbreak by placing Wuhan and nearby cities under a de-facto quarantine encompassing roughly 50 million people in Hubei province.

This quarantine has since been lifted, as authorities watch to see whether cases will rise again. The US and many other European countries are now the new epicentre of the Covid-19 outbreak. In Italy, where the death toll surpassed that of China, the government took the unprecedented step of extending a lockdown to the entire country, shutting cinemas, theatres, gyms, discos, pubs and banning funerals and weddings. In the UK, the government has shut schools, pubs, restaurants, bars, cafés and all non-essential shops for at least six weeks.

One wonders what the hotels and restaurants would do during this very long period of lockdown.

Going back into operation in a new environment would surely bring with it many unexpected challenges. Between figuring out social distancing protocols and mitigating the risk throughout the property, we are certain to face tough times in the coming months and years.

The landscape changed rapidly and while no one can say with any degree of certainty where everything will land, we will see the shape of things to come. Reduced capacity allowance in restaurants and bars, queuing for entry into stores, wearing a mask all day, sanitising the hands and temperature checks by security guards at entrances to any store, at least in Asia.

One of the challenges include finding new sources of revenue. Creative ideas for driving revenue have always been the expectation but a prolonged downturn and slow recovery will put immense pressure on the entire system. Owners and managers have to put their thoughts together and finding ways to leverage on what is already in place and analyse a new way forward.

There will undoubtedly be more changes to come as the situation evolves.

Yes, and as I end this, hopes have been raised with some rushed vaccines for Covid and there seems to be optimism. At the same time new strains seem to be emerging as well. One can only hope it all ends soon and the world gets back to its feet again.

A meaningful retirement

I must say that my time in the hotel industry had been rewarding, fun and challenging. I am glad my time passed without major hiccups.

I was at the right place at the right time. If you love to serve various nationalities and customers with different demands and behaviours (including employees) and spend long hours under the pressure from the management and owners, this is definitely the industry to be in. This is where you can see the world and experience the culture of various countries.

Like many, you've probably spent at least a little time thinking about what to do during retirement.

How will you fill your days? Where will you go? What will you do? With whom will you spend time?

In retirement, you will likely have more options on how to spend your time than ever before. And, you certainly don't have to settle on only one goal, hobby or pursuit. Maybe you'll pursue painting. Or perhaps skydiving if it is more up to your liking?

Retirement for me was rather eventful.

For a start, I renovated the apartment I bought 22 years ago.

I went on 3 extensive holiday trips with friends to experience the vineyards in Spain, the snow and seafood in Hokkaido, a trip on the Volga in Russia (with plenty of vodka and visits to museums).

I visited my family in Switzerland.

I joined the Rotary Club in Kuala Lumpur, was a Hotel Consultant for 1 year and 6 months in Kathmandu, tracked the Annapurna (Himalaya region) while in Nepal.

I took up a photography course and travelled with some enthusiastic photographers to Myanmar, Ethiopia, Norway (for the Northern lights), Malacca, Kuala Terengganu and Kuala Lumpur.

I encountered a very rare opportunity when I met the Royal Family of Bhutan during the wedding ceremony of the niece of the King who married a commoner (our personal guide and friend during our travel in Bhutan, some years back). It was an occasion where no photos were allowed and I had to rent the national dress of the Himalayan Kingdom of Bhutan (the Gho) to blend in with the 150 invited guests.

On top of all that, I joined the International Wine and Food Society in Kuala Lumpur, where I met new friends. I learned the local language (Bahasa Melayu) on Zoom, and visited the gym 3 to 4 times a week.

With lots of time on my hands, I also managed to pen down the countries I have not yet visited.

Top of my list includes Mongolia and South America.

Life often hits us with one thing after another. My former boss reprimands me occasionally for not reaching the revenue target, or an unexpected expense arises in my bank account that puts me in the red zone. Or a family member becomes ill, and setbacks abound that seem almost hostile in nature.

It is hard enough to organise your thoughts as it is, but even harder to find the energy to solve problems. Go for it or just do it as Nike advocates. Sometimes, it seems like we just can't get a break. But the problem really arises when challenges such as this come about. When that happens, we become overwhelmed and are most at risk of quitting on our dreams and goals.

Everyone feels like quitting at some point, get under the blanket and completely ignore everyone and everything.

It happens to the best of us, but know that this 'escape' is temporary. You should allow yourself a break every now and then; you need to recharge in order to start fresh, but never allow that break to last for too long and turn you into a quitter.

Quitting won't make the challenges go away. The only way to truly handle your challenges is by facing them head on – and that requires a powerful, pure, burning motivation to take action despite these setbacks. But where do we get the necessary motivation from?

It is important to have at hand some encouraging quotes or a few uplifting sayings. You might underestimate their effect, but reading some can do magic in your current situation. They work like a pill that helps you get back on track and face your challenges with new energy.

Motivational quotes have proven themselves to be quite beneficial for many people. They inspire and remind me that 'I got this'. It's amazing how a few words can give us such energy.

And in closing, I would like to leave you with some of my favourite quotes:

> *'In our lives, change is unavoidable, loss is unavoidable. In the adaptability and ease*

with which we experience change, lies our happiness and freedom.' -Gautama Buddha-

'The secret of health for both mind and body is not to mourn for the past, worry about the future, or anticipate troubles, but to live in the present moment wisely and earnestly'. -Gautama Buddha-

'Money doesn't bring happiness and creativity. Your creativity and happiness bring money.' -William Feather-

Hardly the day started and ... it is already 1 p.m.
Barely arrived on Monday and it is already Tuesday
... and the month is already over.
... and the year is almost up.
... and already 40, 50, or 60 years of our lives have passed.
... and we realise that we lost our parents, friends.
and we realise that it is too late to go back ...
So ... Let's try, however, to take full advantage of the time we have left ...
Let's not stop looking for activities that we like ...
Let's put colour in our greyness ...
Let's smile at the little things in life that put balm in our hearts.
And yet, we must continue to enjoy serenely the time that remains. Let's try to eliminate the 'after' ...
I do it after ...
I will say after ...
I will think about it after ...
We leave everything for later as if 'after' was ours.
Because what we do not understand is that:
after, the coffee cools ...
after, priorities change ...
after, the charm is broken ...
after, health passes ...
after, the children grow up ...
after, the parents get older ...
after, the promises are forgotten ...
after, the day becomes the night ...
after, life ends ...
And after that, it's often too late...
So ... leave nothing for later ...
Because always waiting for later, we can lose the best moments,
the best experiences,
the best friends,
the best family,
The day is today ...
The moment is now ...

-A favourite message from an unknown source-

From my Childhood in Switzerland to the most known and established Hotel School in Lausanne and a visit to Cornell University Ithaca.

From Waiter to Cook to Hotel General Manager in local and International Hotel chains in Asia.

The Technology and booking pattern over the years changed at the speed of light.

From traditional brochures to direct Hotel bookings, various OTA's and Social Media platforms.

An increasing pool of distribution channels has become available. Every booking implies a solid commission. Increase direct traffic to your Hotel. (Be visible and competitive)

Many Employers across the board are looking for professionals with a combination of both hard and soft skills, cultural integration, multitasking, excellent customer service and communication, it is paramount to show team spirit, positive attitude and a carrying personality.

Today's Covid-19 crisis has underlined the global importance of the travel and tourism industry economically as well as its interconnection with other related industries

From small and large tour operators to regional and multinational hotel chains and to major airlines, everyone in the industry has been impacted by the border travel restriction as well as complete lockdown.

What will hospitality leaders do today, to remain competitive in this ever so challenging market? Entrepreneurial and creational thinking is priority to keep afloat. Change the overall approach by 360 degrees.

My Parents

Siblings & Immediate Family Members

Hotel School Lausanne, Switzerland

Team, Mandarin Oriental, Manila

Basel, Switzerland

Swiss Army

President Rotary Club of Gombak

President Rotary International, 2019/20

My Time In Bangkok

IBEROTEL Palace, Sharm el-Sheikh, Egypt

Moevenpick, Phuket

Staff Party Moevenpick Phuket

Wedding Ceremony, Buthan

Hotel Owners
DUSIT Princess Kathmandu, Nepal

Fitness First

Essential needs to be a Manager